Schaum's Quick Guide
to Writing Great Research Papers

311

Schaum's Quick Guide to Writing Great Research Papers

Laurie Rozakis, Ph.D.

The State University of New York
Farmingdale State College

Second Edition

McGraw-Hill

New York   Chicago   San Francisco   Lisbon   London   Madrid
Mexico City   Milan   New Delhi   San Juan   Seoul
Singapore   Sydney   Toronto

The *McGraw·Hill* Companies

2 3 4 5 6 7 8 9 0   DOC/DOC   0 1 3 2 1 0 9 8

ISBN 978-0-07-148848-8
MHID 0-07-148848-0

This book was set in Stone Serif by International Typesetting and Composition.

McGraw-Hill books are available at special quantity discounts for use as premiums and sales promotions, or for use in corporate training programs. For more information, please write to the Director of Special Sales, McGraw-Hill Professional, Two Penn Plaza, New York, NY 10121-2298. Or contact your local bookstore.

Library of Congress Cataloging-in-Publication Data

Rozakis, Laurie.
    Schaum's quick guide to writing great research papers / Laurie Rozakis.—2nd ed.
       p.   cm.
    Includes bibliographical references and indexes.
    ISBN-13: 978-0-07-148848-8
    ISBN-10: 0-07-148848-0
    1. Report writing.   2. Research.   I. Title.   II. Title: Quick guide to writing great research papers.
    LB1047.3.R69   2007
    808'.02—dc22   2006103423

Contents

Schaum's Quick Guide
to Writing Great Research Papers

Part I

Getting Started

Chapter 1

What is a Research Paper?

Research is a way of life dedicated to discovery.
—ANONYMOUS

Few of us are ever going to become professional researchers, but *all* of us will find times when research is indispensable to our lives. Whether you're looking for information about a car's safety record, a community's schools, or a company's stocks, you'll need to know how to gather, sort, and track the facts and opinions available to you.

That's why you need to know how to do a research paper. A research paper is such a useful and efficient method of gathering and presenting reliable information that preparing one is frequently assigned in high school, college, and graduate school. It shows your instructor that you can gather, evaluate, and synthesize information—in short, that you can think.

In addition, research papers are often important in business, especially in fast-changing fields where facts and opinions must be sorted. These businesses include law, manufacturing, retailing, security, fashion, computer technology, banking, insurance, and accounting.

Definition of the Research Paper

A *research paper* presents and argues a *thesis,* the writer's proposition or opinion. It is an analytical or persuasive essay that evaluates a position. As such, a research paper tries to convince readers that the writer's argument is valid or at least deserves serious consideration. Therefore, a research paper requires the writer to be creative in using facts, details, examples, and opinions to support a point. The writer has to be original and inventive in deciding what facts will best support the thesis and which ones are superfluous.

When you write a research paper, you have to read what various recognized authorities have written about the topic and then write an essay in which you draw your own conclusions about the topic. Since your thesis is fresh and original, you won't be able to merely summarize what someone else has written. Instead, you'll have to synthesize information from many different sources to create something that is your own.

A research paper is *not*

- just a collection of facts on a topic
- a summary of information from one or more sources
- merely reporting what others have said
- expository or descriptive

For example, here is how typical college-level topics could be developed for research papers.

Topic	Suitable for a Research Paper Because It Argues a Point	Not Suitable for a Research Paper Because It Doesn't Argue a Point
Taxes	A flat tax should replace our current system of graduated rates of taxation.	Survey of different methods of taxation
Testing	Standardized tests are an accurate measure of success in college.	Different types of standardized tests
School	Year-round school will raise students' achievement.	Survey of topics taught in secondary schools
Thomas Hardy	Thomas Hardy is the greatest English novelist of his era.	Chronology of Hardy's life and writing

4

What are the Qualities of a Good Research Paper?

No matter what the topic or length, all effective research papers meet the following ten criteria:

1. Successful papers stay tightly focused on their *thesis*, the point they are arguing.
2. The paper shows that the writer has a strong understanding of the topic and source material used.
3. The paper shows that the writer has read widely on the topic, including the works of recognized authorities in the field.
4. The paper includes an acknowledgement of the opposition but shows why the point being argued is more valid.
5. Proof for the paper's thesis is organized in a clear and logical way.
6. Each point is supported by solid, persuasive facts and by examples.
7. The work is original, not plagiarized. Every outside source is carefully documented.
8. All supporting material used in preparation of the paper can be verified.
9. The paper follows a specific format, including the use of correct documentation and a Works Cited page.
10. The paper uses standard written English. This is the level of diction and usage expected of educated people in high schools, colleges, universities, and work settings.

Time Management

Whether you're writing a research paper as a class assignment or as part of a work-related assignment, the odds are very good that you're not going to have all the time you want. In nearly every case, you'll be working against a deadline. You'll have to produce a paper of a certain length by a certain date.

Since you're working under pressure within narrow constraints, it's important to know how to allocate your time from the very beginning of the process. In fact, one of the most challenging aspects of writing a research paper is planning your time effectively. You don't want to end up spending the night before the paper is due downloading inferior material from second-rate Web sites and keyboarding until you're bleary-eyed. Your paper will be a disaster—and you'll be wiped out for days.

No one deliberately plans to leave work to the last minute, but few novice writers (and even some more experienced ones!) realize how much time it takes to select a topic, find information, read and digest it, take notes, and write successive drafts of the paper. This is especially true when you're faced with all the other pressures of school and work. No one can produce a good research paper without adequate time.

That's why it is crucial to allocate your time carefully from the day you get the assignment. Before you plunge into the process, start by making a plan. Below are some plans to get you started. Each plan assumes a five-day workweek, so you can relax on the weekends.

Notice that the last step is "wiggle room." When it comes to any major project such as a research paper, things can often go wrong. Perhaps the authoritative book you really need is out of the library and it will take too long to get it from another library, so you'll have to rely more heavily on other sources, which means more time doing research than you had counted on. Or maybe you lost some of your bibliography cards, the dog ate your rough draft, or your hard drive crashed.

SAMPLE SCHEDULES

Several sample schedules for different time periods are given below.

4-Week Plan (20 Days)

If you have 4 weeks (20 days) in which to complete a research paper...

Task	Time
1. Selecting a subject	1/2 day
2. Narrowing the subject into a topic	1/2 day
3. Crafting a thesis statement	1/2 day
4. Doing preliminary research	2 days
5. Taking notes	2 days
6. Creating an outline	1/2 day
7. Writing the first draft	3 days
8. Finding additional sources	2 days
9. Integrating source materials	1 day
10. Using internal documentation	1/2 day
11. Creating a Works Cited page	1/2 day
12. Writing front matter/end matter	1 day
13. Revising, editing, proofreading	3 days
14. Keyboarding	1 day
15. Wiggle room	2 days

6-Week Plan (30 Days)

If you have 6 weeks (30 days) in which to complete a research paper...

Task	Time
1. Selecting a subject	1 day
2. Narrowing the subject into a topic	1 day
3. Crafting a thesis statement	1 day
4. Doing preliminary research	3 days
5. Taking notes	3 days
6. Creating an outline	1 day
7. Writing the first draft	4 days
8. Finding additional sources	3 days
9. Integrating source materials	2 days
10. Using internal documentation	1 day
11. Creating a Works Cited page	1 day
12. Writing front matter/end matter	1 day
13. Revising, editing, proofreading	4 days
14. Keyboarding	2 days
15. Wiggle room	2 days

8-Week Plan (40 Days)

If you have 8 weeks (40 days) in which to complete a research paper...

Task	Time
1. Selecting a subject	2 days
2. Narrowing the subject into a topic	2 days
3. Crafting a thesis statement	1 day
4. Doing preliminary research	4 days
5. Taking notes	5 days
6. Creating an outline	1 day
7. Writing the first draft	7 days
8. Finding additional sources	3 days
9. Integrating source materials	3 days
10. Using internal documentation	2 days
11. Creating a Works Cited page	1 day
12. Writing front matter/end matter	1 day
13. Revising, editing, proofreading	4 days
14. Keyboarding	2 days
15. Wiggle room	2 days

12-Week Plan (60 Days)

If you have 12 weeks (60 days) in which to complete a research paper, remember that longer is not necessarily better. With a long lead time, it's very tempting to leave the assignment to the last minute. After all, you do have *plenty* of time. But "plenty of time" has a way of evaporating fast. In many instances, it's actually easier to have less time in which to write a research paper, because you know that you're under pressure to produce.

If you have 12 weeks (60 days) in which to complete a research paper...

Task	Time
1. Selecting a subject	3 days
2. Narrowing the subject into a topic	2 days
3. Crafting a thesis statement	1 day
4. Doing preliminary research	8 days
5. Taking notes	8 days
6. Creating an outline	2 days
7. Writing the first draft	10 days
8. Finding additional sources	4 days
9. Integrating source materials	3 days
10. Using internal documentation	2 days
11. Creating a Works Cited page	1 day
12. Writing front matter/end matter	2 days
13. Revising, editing, proofreading	6 days
14. Keyboarding	3 days
15. Wiggle room	5 days

Chapter 2

How Do I Choose a Subject for My Research Paper?

> *Writing is no trouble: you just jot down ideas as they occur to you. The jotting is simplicity itself—it is the occurring which is difficult.*
>
> —STEPHEN LEACOCK

This book presents a clear, effective, and proven way to write a fine research paper. The steps are arranged in chronological order, from start to finish. Be aware, however, that writers rarely move in such neat steps. While it is strongly recommended that you follow the steps in order, don't worry if you find yourself repeating a step, doing two steps at the same time, or skipping a step and then returning to it.

For example, let's say that you choose a subject, narrow it to a topic, and create a thesis statement. Then you set off to find the information you need. Once you start looking at sources, however, you discover that there is too much material on the topic or not enough material on the topic. In this case, you might go back to the previous step and rework your thesis to accommodate your findings and the new direction your work has taken. Of course, you always have the option of sticking with your original thesis and creating the research material you need. More on this in Chapter 7.

Here's another common occurrence. You think you have found all the material you need and so you start writing. But part way through your first draft, you find that you're missing a key piece of information, a crucial fact, an essential detail. To plug the hole, you'll go back and find the material—even though you are, in effect, repeating a step in the process. That's fine.

The process presented in this book is effective, but remember that one size may not fit all. As a result, you may find yourself adapting the information here to fit your particular writing style. Now, turn to the first step in the process of writing a research paper, *selecting a subject.*

> The *subject* of a research paper is the general content. Subjects are broad and general.

Step 1: Brainstorm Subjects

Sometimes, your teacher, professor, or supervisor will assign the subject for your research paper. In these cases, you usually have very little choice about what you will write. You *may* be able to stretch the subject a bit around the edges or tweak it to fit your specific interests, but most often you will have to follow the assignment precisely as it was given. To do otherwise means risking failure, since the instructor was precise in the assignment.

However, in other cases, you will be instructed to develop the subject and topic on your own. Very often, this is part of the research paper process itself, for it teaches you to generate ideas and evaluate them. It helps you learn valuable decision-making skills in addition to writing and research methods.

Choosing a subject for a research paper calls for good judgment and solid decision-making skills. Experienced writers know that the success or failure of a research paper often depends on the subject; even the best writers find it difficult (if not impossible) to create a winning paper around an unsuitable subject.

The right subject can make your paper; the wrong one can break it. Unsuitable subjects share one or more of the following characteristics:

- They cannot be completed within the time allocated.
- They cannot be researched since the material does not exist.
- They do not persuade since they are expository or narrative.
- They are trite, boring, or hackneyed.
- They are inappropriate, offensive, or vulgar.

> Nearly every subject *can* be researched, but not every subject *should* be researched.

There are a number of reasons for this. For example, why bother researching a subject that many others have done before you? Trite, shopworn, and boring subjects often lead to trite, shopworn, and boring research papers. Give yourself (and your teacher) a break by starting with a fresh, exciting subject.

As a result, it's important to think through a subject completely before you rush into research and writing. In addition, your writing will be better if your subject is suitable for your readers and purpose.

Where can you get ideas for research paper subjects? You have two main sources: *yourself* or *outside experts*. Let's start with what you already know.

START WITH YOUR OWN IDEAS AND INTERESTS

All writing begins with thinking. When you come up with a subject for a research paper, as with any other writing assignment, you must draw upon yourself as a source. All writers depend on their storehouse of experience—everything they have seen, heard, read, and even dreamed.

People often worry that they have nothing to write about, especially when it comes to a mammoth project such as a research paper. Often, however, you know far more than you are willing to give yourself credit for. Your task? To discover which of your ideas will be most suitable for the research paper you have to do now. Below are some proven techniques for generating subjects.

Since not every method works for every writer, experiment with these techniques to find the one or ones that suit your writing style. And even if one method works very well for you, don't be afraid to try other ones. They may uncover still other possible subjects for your research paper.

1. **Keep an idea book.** Many professional writers keep an "idea book" as a place where they can store their ideas and let them incubate. You don't have to be a professional writer to use an idea book; it works equally well for novice writers. Think of this as a scrapbook rather than as a diary or journal. Here are some items that can serve as the seeds for a great research paper:

   - newspaper clippings
   - personal letters
   - postcards
   - magazine articles
   - snapshots
   - other visuals

2. **List ideas.** You can also brainstorm ideas for possible subjects. This method allows you to come up with many ideas fast because you're writing words, not sentences or paragraphs. To use this method, number from 1 to 10 and jot down any ideas you have for research paper subjects. Here's a sample:

   1. immigration
   2. vegetarianism
   3. eating disorders
   4. sport utility vehicles
   5. sealed adoption records
   6. Affirmative Action
   7. divorce laws
   8. censorship of novels
   9. Salem witchcraft trials
   10. mutual funds

3. **Make a web.** Webbing, also called "clustering" or "mapping," is a visual way of sparking ideas for subjects. Since a web looks very different from a paragraph or list, many writers find that it frees their mind to roam over a wider variety of ideas.

   When you create a web, first write your subject in the center of a page. Draw a circle around it. Next draw lines radiating from the center and circles at the end of each line. Write an idea in each circle. Here's a model:

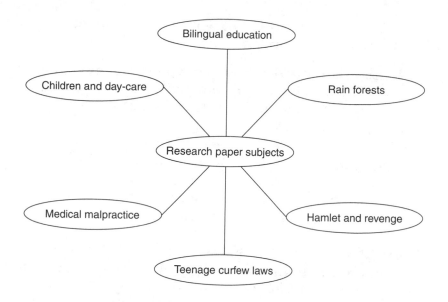

4. **Draw visuals.** A web is only one type of visual format; there are many other visuals that you can use to generate ideas for research paper subjects. Charts work especially well for some people; Venn diagrams or story charts for others. Experiment with different visual formats until you find which ones work best for you in each writing situation.

5. **Use the 5 Ws and H.** The "5 Ws and H" stand for *who, what, when, where, why,* and *how.* They are also called "The Journalist's Questions" because they appear in the first paragraph (the "lead") of every news story. Asking these questions forces you to approach a subject from several different angles. Many people find this approach useful for starting highly detailed papers.

6. **Freewrite.** *Freewriting* is nonstop writing that helps jog your memory and release hidden ideas. When you freewrite, you jot down whatever comes to mind without worrying about spelling, punctuation, grammar, or style. Select the method of composition that allows you to freewrite most quickly: keyboarding or longhand. The

key to freewriting is letting your mind roam and seeing what subjects it uncovers.

7. **Read.** Reading widely can help you come up with great research paper topics. Try different genres to get ideas. Don't restrict yourself. Here are some possibilities:

   - short stories
   - essays
   - newspapers
   - professional journals
   - autobiographies
   - plays and drama

   - novels
   - poems
   - magazines
   - critical reviews
   - biographies
   - scripts

CONSULT EXPERTS FOR SUBJECTS

Can't come up with anything you like? Why not consult outside experts? In addition to speaking to people who have written research papers, check with the teachers, parents, and professionals you know. Doctors, lawyers, accountants, real estate salespeople, computer programmers, and other business people are all excellent sources for ideas.

Step 2: Consider Your Parameters

If you are asked to develop your own subject for a research paper, how can you decide which of the subjects you have brainstormed shows the most promise? Start with these four guidelines:

1. **Time.** The amount of time you have to write influences every writing situation, but especially when it comes to writing a research paper. Since there are so many aspects of this situation that are out of your control—such as availability of research materials—it is critical that you select a subject that you can complete in the time you have been allotted.

2. **Length.** The length of the paper is also a factor in your choice of subjects. It will obviously take you much longer to write a 50-page research paper than it will to write a 10-page research paper. Weigh this consideration as you select a

subject. The shorter the paper and the longer the time you have to write, the more leeway you have to select a challenging subject.

3. **Research.** The type of research you use also determines the subject you select. For instance, if your assignment specifies that you use primary sources, such as letters, interviews, and eyewitness accounts, you might not wish to do a paper on Shakespeare, since there are relatively few primary sources available and they are difficult to read. Conversely, if your assignment specifies that you use secondary sources such as critical reviews, a paper on one of Shakespeare's plays would be very suitable.

4. **Sources.** The number of sources you must use and their availability is also a factor in your choice of a subject. If you have access to a major university library with a million or more volumes and extensive free databases, you're probably going to find the material you need. But if you don't have an extensive library in your area or access to high-quality databases, it might be much harder for you to get the secondary material you need. In this case, you might want to consider a subject that requires more primary sources such as experiments, interviews, and surveys. See Chapter 5 for a full discussion of primary and secondary sources.

Step 3: Evaluate Subjects

You shouldn't select a subject hastily, but neither should you spend too much time sifting through ideas. Here are six guidelines to make the process easier:

1. **Consider your *purpose*.** With a research paper, your purpose is to convince. Persuasive writing succeeds in large part because it has such a clear sense of purpose. Keep your purpose in mind as you weigh the suitability of various subjects. If you can't slant the subject to be persuasive, it isn't a good choice for a research paper.

2. **Focus on your audience.** As you select a subject, always focus on your *audience*—the person or people who will be reading your paper. Always remember that you're writing for a specific audience. Tailor your subject to suit your audience's expectations and requirements. Don't select a subject that condescends to your readers, offends them, or panders to them. Don't try to shock them, either—it always backfires.

3. **Select a subject you like.** If you have a choice, try to select a subject that interests you. Since you will be working with the subject for weeks and even months, you will find the process of writing your research paper much more enjoyable if you like the subject matter you have selected.

   Start with hobbies, sports, favorite courses, career plans, and part-time jobs. For example, if you're interested in computers, you may wish to persuade your readers of the negative effects of computers on children. You might argue that we are raising a generation of sedentary children as a result of an over-emphasis on computer skills and the abundance of computer games.

   School courses can also be an excellent source of topics for your research paper. If your favorite class is physical education, consider a persuasive paper related to the subject. For instance, persuade your readers that physical education classes should be mandatory in grades K–12.

   What happens if you have been assigned a subject you detest? See if you can find an aspect of the subject that you like. Of course, always check all changes with your instructor before you begin to write.

4. **Be practical.** Even though you want to choose a subject that appeals to you, look for subjects that have sufficient information available, but not so much information that you can't possibly read it all. Writing a research paper is challenging enough without making the task that much harder for yourself. For instance, avoid research papers on the entire Civil War, U.S. transportation system, or modern

American literature. These subjects are simply too vast to be covered in a research paper; they require a book-length dissertation.

5. **Beware of "hot" subjects.** "Hot" subjects—very timely, popular issues—often lack the expert attention that leads to reliable information. The web pages, books, articles, and interviews on such subjects have often been produced in great haste. As a result, they are not carefully fact-checked. In addition, such research papers get stale *very* quickly—sometimes, the issue can seem dated even before you finish writing the paper.

   The media *can* be an excellent source of research paper subjects, especially newspapers, magazines, radio shows, and web sites. But rather than focusing on the side everyone else sees, probe a little deeper for the story behind the story. This can help you avoid getting trapped in a subject that's here today but gone tomorrow.

6. **Recognize that not all questions have answers.** When you write a research paper, you are attempting to find an answer to the question you have posed or the one that has been given to you. Remember that not all research questions lead to definitive answers. Rather, many questions invite informed opinions based on the evidence you have gathered from research. Dealing with questions that don't have definitive answers can make your paper provocative and intriguing.

   Now that you have learned how to choose a subject, we'll turn to the crucial issues of narrowing the subject to a topic. You will discover why this is such a crucial step in a successful research paper.

Chapter 3

How Do I Narrow My Subject into a Research Topic? (and Why!)

Writing is just having a sheet of paper, a pen, and not a shadow of an idea of what you're going to say.

—Francoise Sagan

In virtually all cases, your next step is narrowing the subject you have chosen into a topic. This means you find smaller aspects within the subject to be your topic and the basis of your research paper. For instance, sometimes you choose or are assigned a subject that is very broad. How can you deal with this challenge? You narrow the subject into a topic. Other times, the subject is the appropriate scope, but not argumentative. In this case as well, you must narrow the subject into a topic that can be argued. In this chapter, you'll learn how to narrow your subject into a research topic.

Subject vs. Topic

First, review the difference between a *subject* and a *topic*. Recall that a *subject* of a research paper is the general content. As you learned in Chapter 2, subjects are broad and general.

Examples of possible subjects for a research paper:

- health
- television
- Revolutionary War
- genetic engineering of foods
- foreign policy
- music
- education
- Charles Dickens
- outsourcing
- big box stores

> The *topic* of a research paper is the specific issue being discussed.

The *topic* of a research paper, in contrast, is the specific issue being discussed. The following chart shows some subjects narrowed into topics for a research paper:

Subjects	Topics
Animal rights	If zoos are cruel rather than educational If testing medical procedures/drugs on animals should be increased or decreased
Education	If K–12 school should be year-round If advanced placement high school classes should be eliminated
English	If English should be America's official language If bilingual education is valid
Gambling	If casino gambling should be made illegal in the United States Whether compulsive gambling is a disease, not a moral weakness
Health	Whether the government should increase funding for rare, so-called "orphan" diseases If hepatitis testing should be mandated for all healthcare workers
Voting	If the Electoral College should be abolished If voting should be mandatory

Shaping Your Ideas

Every time you narrow a subject into a topic, remember your boundaries and parameters: time, length, audience, and purpose. Keep all other special considerations in mind as well. Always consider what you can handle within the restrictions you have been given—as well as what you would most enjoy writing about for several weeks or months. Follow these guidelines:

1. Start with a general subject that interests you and fits the parameters of the assignment.
2. Phrase the subject as a question.
3. Brainstorm subdivisions of the subject to create topics.
4. Consult different sources for possible subtopics. Possibilities include the Internet, card catalog, reference books, magazines, friends, and the media.
5. Sift the ideas until you find one that suits the assignment, audience, and your preferences.
6. Write your final topic as a question.

Below is the process that Samantha followed to narrow a subject into a topic. Samantha wanted to write a research paper on some aspect of television, a very broad subject.

By looking through the Internet, skimming the card catalog, talking to friends, watching television, and reading some general interest newsmagazines that had articles on the subject, Samantha came up with these ideas:

Subject Television

Question What do I want to find out about television?

Specific Topics   Television as "vast wasteland"
Television as "chewing gum for the mind"
Children and television
Educational television
Cable television
Television documentaries
Golden Age of television
Television and ethnic stereotypes
Sex and violence on television
Amount of television watched and
its effect
Tabloid television

Reading over the list, Samantha realized that some of her ideas were still very broad. For example, "children and television" is large enough to be the subject of a book—or a series of books. The same is true of "television documentaries," "Golden Age of television," and "cable television."

Further, even narrowing down some of these topics might not lead to persuasive essays. "Cable television," for instance, seems better suited to an expository essay that explains the history of the field, its impact on viewers, and so on.

One evening, Samantha was watching reruns of a children's educational television show she had loved years ago when the idea came to her: *Is educational television really educational?* Maybe educational television was indeed beneficial in teaching numbers, letters, and other necessary content—or perhaps it affected children negatively.

Now Samantha had her narrowed topic and could continue with the next step, writing a thesis statement. This is covered in the next chapter.

Further Examples

Here are some additional examples to study:

Subjects	Topics
Boating	Whether all boaters should be required to earn a license
Eating disorders	If eating disorders such as anorexia and bulimia are caused by the media's emphasis on appearance and weight
Education	Whether college education necessarily prepares student to obtain a well-paying job. And whether or not it should serve this function
Intelligence	Whether intelligence is determined by nature or nurture
Sports	If competitive sports, such as football and basketball, are over-emphasized in American culture
Supreme Court	Whether the Supreme Court is more important than Congress in setting social policy

Checklist

Deciding on a suitable subject and narrowing it down to manageable proportions is crucial to the success of your research paper. How can you decide if you have correctly narrowed your topic? Use this checklist every time you select a topic:

_____ 1. Is my topic *too* limited?

Problem: Sometimes in your zeal to make the topic more precise, you may narrow it so much that you don't have enough left to write about.

Solution: Always remember how many pages you have to fill—say, six pages (1500 words). The overly narrow topic may be just right for a 350–500 word essay, so save it for that assignment. Then find a topic that will fill the length required by the research paper assignment.

_____ 2. Is my topic still too broad?

Problem: You may think you have narrowed your topic sufficiently, but it may still be too vast for the assignment.

Solution: Check your sources. How many pages do they devote to the topic? If it takes other writers a book to answer the question you have posed, your topic is still too big.

_____ 3. Is my topic too technical?

Problem: The topic you have selected is highly technical and you don't have the background to address it.

Solution: Get a new topic. Unless you have the background you need for the topic, you're going to end up spending most of your time filling in the gaps in your knowledge. This is not the time to teach yourself nuclear physics, calculus, or computer programming in C++.

_____ 4. Is my topic stale?

Problem: Everyone seems to know everything about your topic. Who wants to read another paper about legalizing street drugs, euthanasia, or gun control? If your topic bores you before you've even started writing, you can bet it will bore your audience.

Solution: Get a new topic that is fresh and original. A sparkling topic automatically gives you an edge, even if your writing is a little weak.

_____ 5. Is my topic too controversial?

Problem: You fear that you are going to offend your audience with a controversial topic such as abortion, gay marriage, or sex education.

Solution: Don't take the risk. Start with a new topic that suits both your audience and purpose. Papers that shock and offend take unnecessary risks.

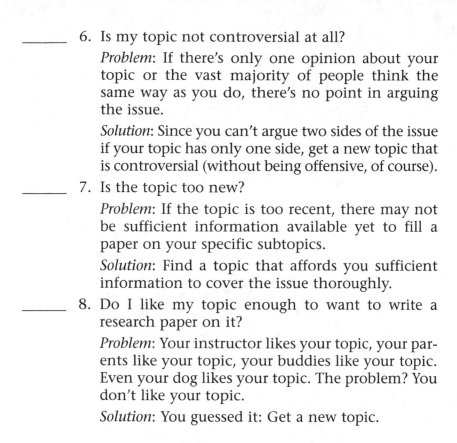

_____ 6. Is my topic not controversial at all?

Problem: If there's only one opinion about your topic or the vast majority of people think the same way as you do, there's no point in arguing the issue.

Solution: Since you can't argue two sides of the issue if your topic has only one side, get a new topic that is controversial (without being offensive, of course).

_____ 7. Is the topic too new?

Problem: If the topic is too recent, there may not be sufficient information available yet to fill a paper on your specific subtopics.

Solution: Find a topic that affords you sufficient information to cover the issue thoroughly.

_____ 8. Do I like my topic enough to want to write a research paper on it?

Problem: Your instructor likes your topic, your parents like your topic, your buddies like your topic. Even your dog likes your topic. The problem? You don't like your topic.

Solution: You guessed it: Get a new topic.

In Chapter 4, you'll explore the next step in the process: writing a thesis statement. This is essential, for everything hinges on your thesis.

How Do I Write a Thesis Statement?

Writing is a deliberate act; one has to make up one's mind to do it.

—JAMES BRITTON

What do you want to discover through your research? In what order will you present your ideas? An effective *thesis statement* is designed to answer these questions. That's why once you have narrowed your topic, it's time to turn your attention to your *thesis statement*. A thesis statement is the central point you are arguing in your research paper.

> A thesis statement is the central point you are arguing in your research paper.

Here are the five basic requirements for a thesis statement:

1. It states the *topic* of the research paper, the main idea.
2. It shows the *purpose* of your essay; in this case, to persuade your readers that your point is valid and deserves serious consideration.
3. It shows the *direction* in which your argument will proceed. A good thesis statement implies (or states) the order in which your ideas will be presented.
4. It is written in focused, *specific language*.
5. It is interesting, showing a clear voice and style.

Since your thesis statement is the backbone of your paper, it's crucial to spend the time to craft exactly the thesis statement you want and need. Here's how to do that.

List Topics

What do you want to know about your subject? What questions do you want answered? Start by listing topics and possible subtopics.

Don't be afraid to make your list long, since your purpose at this point is to see how many subtopics you can generate. In addition, you don't know how much information you can get on each of these subtopics. As a result, your list will likely include specific details as well as broad topics.

Here's how one writer started writing a thesis statement for a research paper on the women's movement.

Topic	Contemporary women and work
Possible subtopics	High-quality education
	Appropriate training
	Pay gap between men and women
	Enormous progress in workforce
	Economic necessity for work
	Women and the "second shift"
	Women's traditional roles
	Women taking "men's jobs"
	Personal satisfaction from work
	Fight against discrimination
	The "glass ceiling"
	Personal ambition
	Restricted jobs/"women's work"
	"Pink-collar jobs"
	"White-collar jobs"
	"Blue-collar jobs"
	Sexual harassment on the job
	Sexual stereotypes about women
	Issue of child care
	Women's movement

By developing and refining your list of subtopics while you're forming your thesis statement, you won't lose time doubling back. But keep in mind that this is a first step— nothing that you write is set in stone.

Having trouble? There are a number of computer software programs available that can help you with this step in your research paper. You may wish to try one and see if it suits your needs.

Draft a Thesis Statement

After you have narrowed your topic and drafted a list of ideas, you're ready to write a preliminary thesis statement. How can you turn this list of subtopics into a thesis statement? Follow these guidelines:

1. Sort the ideas into categories.
2. Select the categories that you want to use.
3. Formulate your thesis around these categories.
4. Write your thesis as a declarative sentence, not a question.
5. Be open to revision.

Follow this pattern: (I expect to prove that) Make an assertion about your topic.

Example
Here's how one writer did it:

Topic	Contemporary women and work
Training	High-quality education
	Appropriate training
Discrimination	The "glass ceiling"
	Pay gap between men and women
	"Pink-collar jobs"
	"White-collar jobs"
	"Blue-collar jobs"
	Women taking "men's jobs"
	Restricted jobs/"women's work"
	Sexual harassment on the job

Reasons women work	Personal satisfaction
	Economic necessity
	Ambition
Pressures	Women and the "second shift"
	Women's traditional roles
	Sexual stereotypes about women
	Issue of child care

Possible Thesis Statements:

- Women won't achieve true equality in the workforce until outmoded sexual stereotypes, discrimination, sexual harassment, and internal and external pressures are eliminated.
- We've come a long way, baby, but women still face significant pressure and discrimination in the workforce.
- With quality education and training, female workers can overcome the discrimination and pressure they face in many jobs.
- Despite pressure and discrimination, women have made great strides in the workforce.
- The women's movement has been instrumental in eliminating much of the discrimination and harassment women face on the job.

Let's look at the first possible thesis statement developed with its main ideas:

Example

Women won't achieve true equality in the workforce until outmoded sexual stereotypes, discrimination, sexual harassment, and internal and external pressures are eliminated.

Thesis: Women have yet to achieve equality in the workforce.

Main points in order:

1. Discrimination must be eliminated.
2. Outmoded sexual stereotypes must be eliminated.
3. Sexual harassment must be eliminated.
4. Internal as well as external pressures must be eliminated.

Research may lead you to revise your thesis, even disprove it, but stating it upfront will point you in the direction of your investigation.

Sample Thesis Statements

Many writers use models to help them shape and evaluate their work. Here are some sample thesis statements that you can use as models for a paper of between 7 and 10 pages. Compare these statements to the one you are writing:

Examples

Too General

Bilingual education isn't effective

On Target

Bilingual education should be eliminated because it limits students' success, burdens students unfairly, and isn't cost-effective.

Too Narrow

Bilingual education helps students maintain their native language

On Target

Bilingual education should be continued because it preserves a students' heritage as well as their native language.

Too General

Rainforests are irreplaceable

On Target

Rain forests must be preserved because they offer people many resources we cannot replace.

Too General

"The Yellow Wallpaper" is a great short story

On Target

The wallpaper in "The Yellow Wallpaper" symbolizes the narrator's suffocating life.

Too Narrow

"Mothers Against Drunk Driving" is an excellent program

On Target

Some programs designed to eliminate drunk driving have been effective, but far more efforts are needed, especially concerning teenager drunk driving.

Too Narrow

A flat tax helps tax accountants

On Target

A flat tax would benefit the government, business, and consumers.

Too General

The cafeteria isn't very good

On Target

The cafeteria could attract more business if it improved the quality of its food, its appearance, and the attitude of the staff.

Check Your Work

Use this checklist to evaluate your thesis statement:

_____ 1. The thesis statement clearly states the main idea of my research paper.

_____ 2. The thesis statement indicates that I am writing a persuasive essay.

_____ 3. If the thesis statement is in response to an assignment, it fulfills the requirements and meets the parameters.

_____ 4. The thesis statement is the appropriate scope for the assignment, neither too broad nor too general.

_____ 5. From the thesis statement, readers can see the order in which my ideas will be presented.

_____ 6. The thesis statement uses specific language rather than vague, general terms.

_____ 7. The thesis statement is interesting, lively, intriguing; it makes my audience want to read the entire paper.

_____ 8. The thesis statement shows evidence of original thought and effort. The topic is fresh and worth my effort to write.

Part II

Doing Research

Chapter 5

How Can I Find the Information I Need?

The beginning of research is curiosity, its essence is discernment, and its goal is truth and justice.
—Isaac H. Satanov

The Information Explosion

We are living in the midst of the greatest explosion of information the world has ever seen. No other generation has been blitzed by the avalanche of books, newspapers, magazines, journals, surveys, advertisements, videos, television shows, movies, maps, charts, graphs, CDs, and tapes that we encounter daily. And that doesn't take into account all the online sources, including Web sites, electronic bulletin boards, Listservs, blogs, newsgroups, and e-mail. More information has been produced in the last *fifty years* than in the previous *five thousand.*

Consider these facts about the amount of information available to us today:

- Fifty thousand books and ten thousand magazines are published every year in America alone.
- Every day, seven thousand scientific studies are written.

- *One* daily edition of the *New York Times* contains more information than an educated person in the sixteenth century absorbed in his or her entire life.
- The amount of information produced doubles *every two years*.

There is so much information that the huge Library of Congress in Washington D.C. has converted and stored all the important information it contains into digital form, "The American Memory." All new information is added to the collection as it is acquired. The information includes written and spoken words, sound recordings, still and moving images, prints, maps, and sheet music that document the American experience—millions of pieces of information. Futurists predict that this onslaught of information will only increase.

What impact do these facts have on you as you prepare your research paper? All the information you need is probably available, but you must know how to locate and sort the useful facts from the useless ones. And with so much out there, knowing how to do research can save you many frustrating hours. Start this process by examining the different kinds of material you can find.

Primary and Secondary Sources

All research can be sorted into two categories: *primary sources* and *secondary sources*. It is important to know the distinction between these two types of sources because they affect how you gather research.

PRIMARY SOURCES

Primary sources are those created by direct observation. The writers were participants or observers in the events they describe. Primary sources include:

- autobiographies
- diaries
- interviews
- historical records and documents

- logs
- eyewitness accounts
- letters
- journals

- oral histories
- photos taken at the scene
- maps prepared by direct observation

- statistics
- surveys
- blogs

SECONDARY SOURCES

Secondary sources were written by people with indirect knowledge. These writers relied on primary sources or other secondary sources for their information. Secondary sources include:

- abstracts
- biographies
- books written by nonparticipants
- encyclopedias
- government documents
- interpretations
- textbooks

- almanacs
- book reviews
- critical analyses
- explanations
- indexes
- literary criticism
- web pages

Primary sources are not necessarily better (or worse) than secondary sources.

Primary Sources:
- provide facts and viewpoints that may not be available from other sources;
- often have an immediacy and freshness that secondary sources lack;
- may be affected by the author's bias.

Secondary Sources:
- may offer a broader perspective than primary sources;
- tend to be less immediate than primary sources;
- may be affected by the author's bias.

Most effective research papers often use a mix of both primary and secondary sources. For example, a research paper on the history of comic books might include primary sources such as interviews with industry editors, artists, and writers as well as their blogs. The writer will also use secondary sources such as web pages, books, magazine articles, and newspaper articles on the subject. This model research paper appears in Chapter 20.

Other topics, in contrast, require more of one type of source material more than the other. A research paper on land use will likely draw data mainly from secondary sources. A paper on bilingual education might use mainly primary sources.

Always check with your instructor before you start your research to see if you must use a specific mix of primary and secondary sources.

You will need to evaluate each source individually, whether it is a primary source or a secondary source. This is covered in detail in Chapter 10.

Basic Search Strategy

Before we get into how to use specific resources, let's cover the general guidelines for research. The following suggestions can make your task easier and less frustrating.

1. **Use key words.** Start by listing key words for your topic that you'll use to search for sources. For example, key words for a research paper on Charlotte Perkins Gilman's *"The Yellow Wallpaper"* might look like this:
   - Gilman, Charlotte Perkins (author)
   - *"The Yellow Wallpaper"* (title)
   - mental illness (a topic in the story)
   - nineteenth-century medicine (another important topic)
   - feminism (a movement that embraced this story)

2. **Include related words.** As you list your key words, think of synonyms that you can use to expand or narrow your search. For example, if the topic of your research paper is overcrowding in national parks, you might include some of these synonyms:
   - environmentalism
   - wilderness
   - national monuments
   - conservation
   - federal lands
   - government lands

Can't think of any synonyms or related terms for your research topic? Check the *Library of Congress Guide to Subject Headings*. This set of reference books identifies the subject headings used by the Library of Congress. It can help you find key words as well as related terms.

3. **Learn the lingo.** Nearly every research tool has an abbreviation—or two. *The Dictionary of Library Biography*, for example, is abbreviated as *DLB; Something About the Author* is called *SATA*. You can learn the abbreviations for print sources by checking the introduction or index. For online sources, check the Help screen.

4. **Know your library.** All libraries offer some special services. Many libraries will get books, newspapers, and magazines for you through interlibrary loans. While there is rarely a charge for this service, it does take time—often as much as two to four weeks. See your reference librarians when you start researching so you know what special services are available, their cost (if any), and the time involved. Be sure to know your library's hours. Of course, get a library card, if you don't have one already.

   Also know which databases your library subscribes to because these proprietary databases contain information that you often cannot access from free sources.

5. **Consult reference librarians.** After reading this guidebook, you should be able to locate nearly every reference source you need on your own. Every once in a while, however, you might get stumped. Maybe you're tired; perhaps you're in an unfamiliar library.

   Whatever the reason, when you have a research question that you can't answer on your own, turn to the reference librarians. They are the experts on research methods and their job is to help you find what you need. In addition, they are very well educated. Most librarians in colleges and universities, for example, are required to have earned two master's degrees, one in information retrieval methods (library science) and one in a subject area (such as English, history, math, and so on).

Many libraries now have live online librarians available 24×7 so you can get your reference questions answered even if the library is closed. You can find this service on your library's home page.

Icons such as this on your library's home page help you access a librarian even when the library is closed.

Checklist of Sources

The list below summarizes the different sources available. Skim it now. As you research, return to the list to help you use a range of sources.

_____ Almanacs

_____ Archival materials (rare books, charts, maps, and so on)

_____ Atlases

_____ Audiovisual materials

_____ Blogs

_____ Books

_____ Databases

_____ Dictionaries (online and print)

_____ E-books (electronic books)

_____ Encyclopedias (online and print)

_____ Essays

_____ Government documents (online and print)

_____ Indexes

_____ Interviews

_____ Magazines (online and print)

_____ Newspapers (online and print)

_____ Online databases

_____ Online card catalog

_____ Pamphlets

_____ Primary sources (letters, diaries, and so on)

_____ Reviews of books, movies, plays, and TV shows

_____ Surveys

_____ Web sites

_____ Yearbooks

Chapter 6

How Do I Use Online Sources?

You should always collect more material than you will eventually use,

—WILLIAM ZINSSER

Radio was around for nearly 40 years before 50 million people decided to tune in. Television was around for 13 years before 50 million viewers got hooked. It took 16 years for 50 million people to buy PCs. How long did it take 50 million people to use the Internet? *Only 4 years.* The Internet is indispensable for research, as millions have discovered. In this chapter, you'll explore some of the most effective techniques for researching on the Internet.

Searching the Web

Unfortunately, the Web is not like a library where information has been arranged within an accepted set of rules. It's more like a garage sale, where items of similar nature are usually grouped together—but not always. As a result, you'll find treasures side-by-side with trash. And like a garage sale, the method of organization on the web shifts constantly.

So how can you search the web for information to use in your research paper? There are several different ways, each of them surprisingly easy. Here's how they work.

SEARCH ENGINES

A *search engine* is a computer program that finds information stored on a computer system such as the World Wide Web. (Search engines have also been designed for corporate and proprietary networks.) The search engine allows the user to ask for content meeting specific criteria and retrieves a list of references that match those criteria.

At the present time, Google is the world's most popular search engine.

Search engines that work with *keywords* help you locate Web sites. You type in a keyword and the search engine automatically looks through its giant databases for matches. The more specific the word or phrase, the better your chances of finding the precise information you need. For example, if you're interested in a college, don't use "college" as a keyword. You'll get millions and millions of responses. Instead, name a specific college, such as "Farmingdale State University." This will send to you the precise web page you need.

Below are the most popular search engines and the dates they began.

Year	Search Engine	Search Engine	Search Engine
1993	Aliweb		
1994	Webcrawler	Infoseek	Lycos
1995	AltaVista	Excite	
1996	Dogpile	Ask Jeeves	Inktomi
1997	Northern Light		
1998	Google		
1999	AlltheWeb	Baidu	
2000	Singingfish	Teoma	Vivisiomo
2003	Info.com	Objects Search	
2004	Yahoo! Search		
2005	MSN Search	Ouaero	
2006	Ask.com (rebranding of Ask Jeeves)	Windows Live Search	

Most web search engines are commercial ventures supported by advertising revenue; as a result, some allow advertisers to pay to have their listings ranked higher in search results. This makes your research more difficult and time-consuming because you have to sift through irrelevant information. Those search engines that don't charge for their results make money by running ads on their pages.

Since not all search engines lead to the same sources, you should use more than one to find the information you need for your research paper. *Bookmark* sources to which you want to return. You can also print out hard copies.

DATABASES

A *database* is a collection of related material stored in a computer in a systematic way so that a computer program can consult it to answer questions. Libraries pay fees to subscribe to specialized databases. You can access these databases in person in the library; increasingly, you can also access these databases for free off-site through the library's portal. The information in these databases has been vetted, so they provide higher-quality information. A library's databases saves you time, too, because you are not sifting through commercial sites, as you do with a search engine.

Subject Area	Databases
Art	ARTstor (high-resolution images of paintings, sculpture, photographs, architecture, and archaeology)
Business	General Reference Center Gold- Gale Business and Company Resource Center Business Source Elite Business Source Premier Reference USA Business & Company ASAP Regional Business News
Education	ERIC
Encyclopedias	Gale Virtual Reference Center Grolier Suite Funk & Wagnalls New World Encyclopedia
Health/Medical	Health and Wellness Resource Center Medline Alternative Health Module Health Source-Consumer Edition Health Reference Center- Academic
History/Politics	History Resource Center History Reference Center
Literature	Boon Review Index Online Contemporary Authors Scribner Writers Series Twayne Authors Series Literature Resource Center
Magazines/Newspapers	EBSCOhost Info Trac OneFile Image Collection General Reference Center Gold New York Times New York Times Historical Archive Newsday Newspaper Source
Music	NAXOS Music Library (online collection of music in streaming media)
Science and Technology	McGraw Hill Encyclopedia of Science & Technology General Science Collection Computer Source

48

WIKIPEDIA

Started in 2001, *Wikipedia* is a free online encyclopedia. Wikipedia is unique because it's written collaboratively by volunteers, allowing most articles to be changed by almost anyone with access to the Web site.

Currently, there are 229 language editions of Wikipedia, 16 of which have more than 50,000 articles each. Wikipedia has more than 5 million articles in many languages, including 1.5 million in English. Wikipedia ranks among the top 20 most visited sites, and many of its pages have been adapted by other sites, such as Answers.com.

A 2005 comparison by the science journal *Nature* of sections of Wikipedia and the *Encyclopedia Brittanica* found that the two were close in terms of the accuracy of their articles on the natural sciences. Nonetheless, there are serious issues over Wikipedia's reliability and accuracy, with the site receiving criticism for the following problems:

- susceptibility to vandalism
- bias
- spoof (fake) articles
- questionable information
- uneven quality and inconsistency
- preference for popularity over credentials
- poor writing
- lack of proper sources to legitimize articles

Wikipedia can be a valuable reference tool, but use it with care. Remember that the articles can be written by anyone: 80-year-old Ph.D.'s to 8-year-old cybergeeks.

Always verify all research information you find in at least two sources.

Newsgroups comprise people interested in a specific topic who share information electronically. You can communicate with them through a *Listserv,* an electronic mailing list for subscribers interested in a specific topic, or through *Usenet,* special-interest newsgroups open to the public.

These sources allow you to keep up with the most recent developments in your area of research and may also point you to useful information and resources that could have taken you a long time to find on your own.

E-MAIL

E-mail, electronic mail, lets you communicate electronically with specific people. Senders and receivers must have e-mail addresses. There are specific programs that act as "phone books" to help you find the person you are looking for.

Great Places on the Web

Below are some useful places to visit on the web as you begin your research.

Note: Every care has been taken to make this list timely and correct. But just as people move, so do Web sites. Since this book was published, the Web site may have moved. In that case, there will be a forward link. If not, use "keyword" to find the new site.

Library of Congress
http://www.lcweb.loc.gov

Encyclopedia Britannica
http://www.britannica.com

U.S. Federal Agencies
http://www.lib.lsu.edu/gov/fedgov.html
http://www.fedworld.gov

Virtual Reference Shelf
http://www.loc.gov/rr/askalib/virtualref.html

Wikipedia
http://wikipedia.org

Reference Desk
http://www.refdesk.com/instant.html

Hints for Searching on the Internet

The Internet presents a vast number of widely distributed resources covering thousands of topics and providing many options for research in many fields. Often there is so much information that you may not know where to begin. Or maybe you haven't been able to locate what you're seeking.

When you do your search, don't expect something that you found today to be there tomorrow—or even an hour later. If you find material and need it, keep a copy of it. It's not enough to write down the address and plan on locating the site later.

One of the best strategies to find a subject on the Internet is to use a **Boolean** search. It uses the terms *and, or,* and *not* to expand or restrict a search. Here's how they work:

and or +   If you tell an electronic search tool to look for *national parks* and *pollution* alone, it will list all the works having to do with either subject. But if you link them with the word *and* or + by typing in "national parks and pollution," the computer will narrow your search to only those sources in which both terms appear.

or –   If you link two terms with "or" or a minus sign (–), the search will lead to all sources that contain either term.

not   Using *not* will also narrow a search. Telling the search engine to look for "national parks not Bryce Canyon," for instance, will lead to all sources about national parks except those mentioning Bryce Canyon.

Relax!

No one is an expert on every facet of the Internet—it's simply impossible. While many people are skilled with the tools and have a good idea where to look for information on many topics, no one can keep up with the information flow. Fortunately, you don't have to understand everything to use the Internet quickly and easily. All you need are a computer and the time to explore different paths.

Chapter 7

How Do I Use Books for My Research Paper?

Be sure you go to the author to get at his meaning, not to find yours.

—John Ruskin

For many people, books are an indispensable part of research. For starters, they're "user-friendly." It's easy to open a book and start reading. You don't need any special equipment such as a computer terminal to read a book, either. Since it takes time to write and publish a book, they tend to be reliable sources, as you will learn in Chapter 12. Right now, you'll learn how to find the books you need to complete your research.

Classification of Books

The books you will use for your research paper fall into two main categories: *fiction* and *nonfiction*.

- *Fiction* is novels and short stories. Fiction is cataloged under the author's last name.
- *Nonfiction books*, however, are classified in two different ways. Some libraries use the Dewey Decimal System; other libraries use the Library of Congress system. In general, elementary, junior high, high school, and community libraries use the Dewey Decimal System. University and academic

libraries use the Library of Congress system. The two systems are very different, as you will discover in this chapter.

You will almost always be using more nonfiction books than fiction books for your research. It's not unusual for a major university library to have over a million books. Even a small community library will often have over 100,000 volumes.

How can you find the books you need? You get to know the Dewey Decimal and Library of Congress classification systems. Knowing how these systems work can help you find the books you need to complete your research.

CALL NUMBERS

Each book in the library is marked with a *call number,* which indicates where the book is located in the library's stacks.

- If you are working in a library with "open stacks" (one where you can roam the book collection yourself), you can copy down the call number and get the book yourself.
- If you are working in a library with "closed stacks," (The stacks are restricted to library personnel.), you must fill out a call slip, hand it in at the call desk, and wait for someone to retrieve the book for you.

Some libraries have a mix of open and closed stacks. Whether the stacks are open or closed, be sure to copy down the call number *exactly* as it appears in the card catalog. Otherwise, it will be very hard—if not impossible—for you to find the book. Don't try to remember all the digits in the number as you rush to the stacks. Instead, jot it down. Most libraries even keep small pencils and scraps of paper next to the card catalog for this purpose.

Today, many libraries allow you to track and reserve the books you need through an online catalog, eliminating the need to jot down call numbers. Then you simply go to the library to pick up the books you ordered. The books may be filed in a separate place for your convenience. Next is the online book catalog from the Farmingdale Public Library.

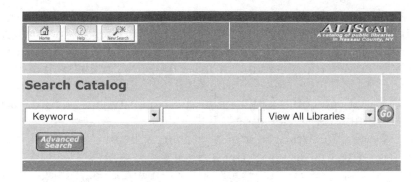

DEWEY DECIMAL CLASSIFICATION SYSTEM

Melvil Dewey (1851–1931) was a man with an obsession for order. This might have made life difficult for his family, but it revolutionized libraries. Before Dewey's system of classifying books was adopted, many libraries relied on systems that filed books by color or size. While working as a librarian at Amherst College, Dewey developed a system that is used today by most elementary schools, high schools, and small public libraries. His classification system, published in 1876, divided nonfiction books into 10 broad categories, as follows:

000–099	General works such as encyclopedias
100–199	Philosophy
200–299	Religion (including mythology)
300–399	Social sciences (including folklore, legends, government, manners, vocations)
400–499	Language (including dictionaries and grammar books)
500–599	Pure science (mathematics, astronomy, chemistry, nature study)
600–699	Technology (applied science, aviation, building, engineering, homemaking)
700–799	Arts (photography, drawing, painting, music, sports)
800–899	Literature (plays, poetry)
900–999	History (ancient, modern, geography, travel)

Each of these categories is further divided for accuracy of classification. For example, 500–599 covers pure science, such as chemistry, astronomy, mathematics, and physics. Books on mathematics can be found from 510–519; geometry is listed under 513. This is further subdivided by decimals to provide additional categories. Additional digits can be added to create even more precise categories.

Books are arranged alphabetically within each classification by the first letter of the author's last name. Therefore, a library that has several books on computer technology will file them all under the same call number but shelve them alphabetically.

LIBRARY OF CONGRESS CLASSIFICATION SYSTEM

The Library of Congress classification system has 20 classes, as follows:

A	General works	M	Music
B-BJ	Philosophy	N	Fine Art
BF	Psychology	P	Language & Literature
BL-BX	Religion	Q	Math, Science, Computer Science
C,D,E,F	History		
G	Geography, Anthropology, Recreation	R	Medicine
		S	Agriculture
		T	Technology, Engineering
H	Social Sciences, Business	U	Military Science
		V	Naval Science
J	Political Science	Z	Bibliography, Printing, Publishing
KF	U.S. Law		
L	Education		

As you noticed, the letters do not necessarily stand for the first letter of the subject they represent. For instance, Political Science is letter J, and Fine Art is letter N.

A Library of Congress call number usually has three parts.

- Part 1: one or two letters for the broad subject area.
- Part 2: numbers and is a further subdivision of the general subject.
- Part 3: a letter and number code for the author's name.

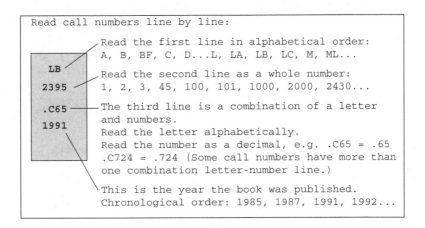

```
Read call numbers line by line:
              Read the first line in alphabetical order:
              A, B, BF, C, D...L, LA, LB, LC, M, ML...
  LB
              Read the second line as a whole number:
  2395        1, 2, 3, 45, 100, 101, 1000, 2000, 2430...
 .C65         The third line is a combination of a letter
              and numbers.
  1991        Read the letter alphabetically.
              Read the number as a decimal, e.g. .C65 = .65
              .C724 = .724 (Some call numbers have more than
              one combination letter-number line.)
              This is the year the book was published.
              Chronological order: 1985, 1987, 1991, 1992...
```

Finding Books on the Shelves

Books are shelved alphabetically by first letter of the first line of the call number, then by the second letter, if any. Here is an example:

Book 1	Book 2	Book 3	Book 4	Book 5	Book 6
B	BF	BT	HV	HV	HV
792	198	1003	541	964	964
.T51	.S2	.M49	.P2	.A42	.A7

Because the Library of Congress system groups related topics together, you can often find unexpected but related avenues to pursue as you research. As a result, leave yourself enough time to browse the shelves as you gather books you need. In addition, many books are now available as e-books, electronic volumes.

Warning!

Unfortunately, library call numbers don't work like the Celsius and Fahrenheit temperature systems. There is no way to convert the call numbers in one system to the call numbers in the other system. This means that you cannot take the call numbers from a library that uses the Dewey classification system to a library that uses the Library of Congress classification system. You'll have to look the book up again if you work between two systems, so it's usually a good idea to pick one library system for books—either the public library system or the university/college library system. Within this system, you can use as many different libraries as you wish, of course.

Using Subject, Title, and Author Searches

There are three different ways that you can find the books you need:

- subject search
- title search
- author search

Your topic determines how you search for a book. Since most research papers deal with topics and issues, you'll likely be searching by subject. However, it is often necessary to look under titles and authors as well. Consider all three avenues of finding information as you look through the card catalog.

Useful Books to Consider

A *reference work* is a compendium of information that you use to find a specific piece of information, rather than read cover to cover. Updated editions are published as needed, in some cases annually. In addition to specific books on your topic, here are some general reference sources to consider:

Encyclopedias. Some teachers will not let their students cite encyclopedias in their bibliographies, but that's no reason not to use them for background information. An encyclopedia can be an excellent way to get a quick, authoritative overview of your topic. This can often help you get a handle on the issues.

There are general encyclopedias (*World Books, Britannica, Colliers, Funk and Wagnalls*) as well as technical ones. The encyclopedias can be in print form or online.

Guide to Reference Sources. Published by the American Library Association, this useful guide has five main categories: general reference works; humanities; social and behavioral sciences; history and area studies; and science, technology, and medicine. The new editions include online sources as well as print ones.

Another excellent reference guide is XReferplus, an online product that accesses more than 200 reference books online.

Who's Who in America. This reference work includes biographical entries on approximately 75,000 Americans and others linked to America. *Who Was Who* covers famous people who have died.

Almanacs. Almanacs are remarkably handy and easy-to-use reference guides. These one-volume books are a great source for statistics and facts. *The World Almanac* and *The Information, Please Almanac* are the two best known almanacs. They are updated every year.

Dictionaries. Complete dictionaries provide synonyms, antonyms, word histories, parts of speech, and pronunciation guides in addition to definitions and spelling. Depending on your topic, you may need to define all terms formally before you begin your research.

Chapter 8

What Other Sources Can I Use for My Research Paper?

Research is the ability to investigate systematically and truly all that comes under your observation in life.

—MARCUS AURELIUS

To get the most reliable, up-to-date, and useful information, you will want to use a variety of different reference sources. As you learned in Chapter 6, the Internet can provide superb research material. However, web pages and commercial sites often have a marked bias. Further, much of the information on the Internet has not been vetted and so is not reliable. As you learned in Chapter 7, books are often an excellent source of material for your research paper. However, books may not be up-to-date since it can take more than a year to write, edit, and publish a book.

Therefore, you will also likely use articles from magazines, newspapers, and journals as well as online sources and books to find information for your research paper. In this chapter, you'll learn how to find magazines, newspapers, and journals as well as interviews, media, and audiovisual sources.

Periodicals: Newspapers/Magazines and Journals

Periodicals include all material that is published on a regular schedule, such as weekly, biweekly, monthly, bimonthly, four times a year, and so on. Newspapers, magazines, and journals are classified as *periodicals*.

- *Newspapers* and *magazines* are aimed at a general readership.
- *Journals* are aimed at a technical audience.

The following chart shows the key differences between newspapers/magazines and scholarly journals.

Characteristic	Newspapers/Magazines	Journals
Author	Professional journalist, everyday person, anonymous author	Expert in the field, scholar, professional writer, professor
References Cited	Usually no bibliography	Includes a bibliography
Editing	Edited by staff	Editorial board or outside scholars review all articles
Audiences	General public	Scholars, researchers, students of the field
Advertisements	Many	Few to none
Appearance	Glossy, many pictures	Not glossy; rarely in color
Frequency	Usually weekly or monthly	Usually monthly or quarterly
Content	General interest articles	Specialized, research based, and aimed at a very specific audience
Language	High school or lower	Technical vocabulary; assumes the reader will have at least an undergraduate degree
Index	Found in general periodical indexes	Found in specialized indexes

The following charts provide examples of the difference in purpose and audience:

Newspaper/Magazine	Audience
Los Angeles Times	General readers
Consumer Reports	People looking to purchase something or evaluate an item
Road and Track	Car owners
Ladies Home Journal	Homemakers

Journal	Audience
American Behavioral Scientist	Psychologists
PMLA (Publication of the Modern Language Association)	Professors and scholars in the humanities
Military Intelligence Professional Bulletin	Army intelligence operatives
JAMA (Journal of the American Medical Association)	Physicians, medical/scientific researchers

Always locate the periodicals that suit your research needs. In university libraries or large community libraries, you locate periodicals in electronic databases. In some instances, you can get the complete article (called "full text"); in other cases, just the citation. Then you have to find the article in another database. A large university library will usually have more than 100 electronic databases and 30,000 full-text electronic journals.

Some of the most common periodical databases are listed in Chapter 6. They include the following:

- EBSCOhost
- Info Trac OneFile
- Image Collection
- General Reference Center Gold
- *New York Times*
- *Newsday*
- Newspaper Source

Original Research

Although you'll probably conduct most of your research online or in the library, remember that there's a great deal of material you can find in laboratories, in courthouses, and in private archives. Consider the possibility of conducting some original research for your research paper. You can do this by interviewing knowledgeable people and devising and distributing questionnaires or surveys. This may be required in class, so always check with your instructor.

INTERVIEWS

Interviews allow you to conduct primary research and acquire valuable information unavailable in print and online sources. By including quotations from people who have direct knowledge of a particular subject, you add considerable authority and immediacy to your paper. You can conduct interviews by telephone, by e-mail, or in person.

Who should you interview? Include only respected people in the field. Don't waste your time with cranks and people with private agendas to further.

Also:

- Be sure to call and confirm the interview.
- Prepare a series of questions well in advance of the interview. The questions should all focus on your topic and the person's recognized area of expertise.

- After the interview, write a note thanking the person for his or her time.
- Get the person's permission *beforehand* if you decide to tape-record or videotape the interview.
- Also obtain a signed release for the right to use their remarks on the record.

SURVEYS

Surveys are useful when you want to measure the behavior or attitudes of a fairly large group. On the basis of the responses, you can draw some conclusions. Such generalizations are usually made in quantitative terms: "Fewer than one-third of the respondents said that they favored further governmental funding for schools," for example. If you decide to create a survey, follow these guidelines:

- Be sure to get a large enough sampling to make your results fair and unbiased. Include at least 50 people, but more is better.
- Don't ask loaded questions that lead people toward a specific response. Be sure that your questions are neutral and unbiased.
- To get honest answers to your questions, it is essential to guarantee your respondents' anonymity. Written surveys are best for this purpose.
- Make the form simple and easy. Few people are willing to take the time to fill out a long, complex form.
- Carefully tabulate your results. Check your math.

In addition, many topics have been extensively discussed by experts on respected television news programs and documentaries. It is often possible to write to the television station and obtain printed transcripts of the programs. You might also be able to videotape the programs or borrow copies of the programs that have already been recorded.

Audiovisual Sources

In addition, you may be able to use audiovisual sources for your research paper. These include:

- DVDs and videotapes
- audiocassettes
- slides
- photographs
- fine art, such as reproductions of paintings and posters

You can often borrow audiovisual materials from your library as you would books, magazines, and other print sources.

Other Sources of Information

You're not done yet! The library has even more sources for you to consider. These include government documents, pamphlets, and special collections.

GOVERNMENT DOCUMENTS

Who's the largest publisher in the United States? It's the government! The government publishes numerous pamphlets, reports, catalogs, and newsletters on most issues of national concern. Government documents are often excellent research sources because they tend to be factual and unbiased. To find government documents, try these online indexes:

- *Monthly Catalog of the United States Government Publications*
- *United States Government Publications Index*

Most government offices have extensive online sites where you can download an astonishing treasure of information, including the full text of many documents and research papers. You can locate these sources through government search engines. Among the best are:

- GPO Access Home Page   http://www.gpoaccess.gov
- About Government   http://www.gpo.gov

PAMPHLETS

Pamphlets are another reference source to consider. They are published by private organizations and government agencies. Since pamphlets are usually too small to place on the shelves, they are stored in the **vertical file**. This is just what the name implies: a filing cabinet with pamphlets arranged in files. *The Vertical File Index: A Subject and Title Index to Selected Pamphlet Material* lists many of the available titles. In addition, you can simply browse in the vertical file under your topic.

SPECIAL COLLECTIONS

Many libraries also have special collections of rare books, manuscripts, newspapers, magazines, photographs, maps, and items of local interest. These are stored in a special room or section of the library. Often you will need permission to access these materials.

Chapter 9

How Do I Track My Research?

Research means to give each and every element its final value by grouping it in the unity of an organized whole.
—Pierre T. DeChardin

As you start to gather your information, you'll need a systematic way to organize it. What you want is an organized list of sources, a *bibliography*. You'll use this list to locate sources and, as you write your research paper, to document the information you used. In this chapter, you'll learn how to make a working bibliography.

Making Bibliography Cards

As you find each source on your topic, you'll want to record publication and location information. When you first start researching, you may just print this information from electronic sources and indexes. Later, you'll turn it into bibliography cards written in the appropriate format.

To do so, get a pack of 3 × 5 index cards. Use one card per source. These are your *bibliography cards*. Cards allow you to keep the most promising sources and discard the irrelevant ones at your convenience. Also, cards can be easily arranged in alphabetical order when the time comes to type a Works Cited page for inclusion at the end of your paper.

There are several different *bibliographic styles*, or ways of documenting sources. As you write your bibliography cards, follow the documentary style assigned by your instructor or preferred by the discipline in which you are writing. For instance:

- Use the *Modern Language Association* (MLA) style for research papers in the humanities, including literature, history, the arts, and religion.
- Use the *American Psychological Association* (APA) style for research papers in the social sciences, such as psychology and sociology.

For sample MLA citations, see Chapter 17.

Bibliography Cards

What should you include on your bibliography cards? Follow the following models.

ELECTRONIC SOURCES

On your card, note the URL (electronic address), the date of your search, and the title.

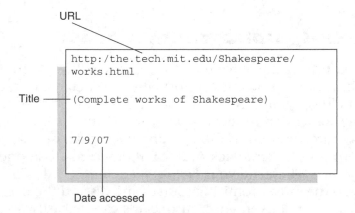

PERIODICALS

On the bibliography card, include the title of the article, title of the periodical, date of the article, author (if available), page numbers (if available), and web address. You may also want to note the number of words, if listed. This tells you the length of the article so you can estimate how much information you are likely to get from it.

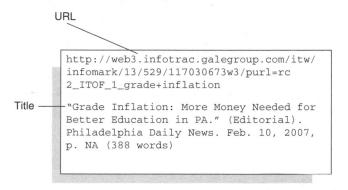

URL

Title ——— "Grade Inflation: More Money Needed for Better Education in PA." (Editorial). Philadelphia Daily News. Feb. 10, 2007, p. NA (388 words)

```
http://web3.infotrac.galegroup.com/itw/
infomark/13/529/117030673w3/purl=rc
2_ITOF_1_grade+inflation
```

BOOKS

On the bibliography card, note anything you are going to need to retrieve the book. Relevant information includes the call number, author or editor, title, place of publication, publisher, date, and library where you found the book. This last detail is very important, since it can save you a great deal of time and effort if you are using more than one library.

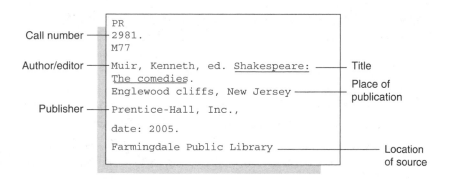

Call number ——— PR 2981. M77

Author/editor ——— Muir, Kenneth, ed. Shakespeare: —— Title
The comedies.
Englewood cliffs, New Jersey —— Place of publication

Publisher ——— Prentice-Hall, Inc.,

date: 2005.

Farmingdale Public Library ——— Location of source

On these cards, include the name of the person you interviewed, the person's area of expertise, the person's address and telephone, and the date of the interview.

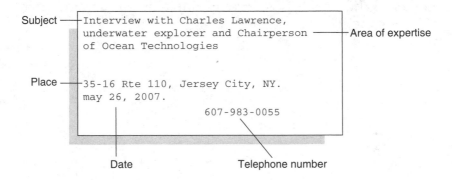

Subject — Interview with Charles Lawrence, underwater explorer and Chairperson — Area of expertise
of Ocean Technologies

Place — 35-16 Rte 110, Jersey City, NY. may 26, 2007.

607-983-0055

Date   Telephone number

Warning!

If a catalog or index does not provide complete bibliographic information, leave blanks that you can fill in later when you have the actual source.

Creating Bibliography Cards on the Computer

Some people prefer to make their bibliography cards on a computer. This method has several advantages.

- You can update, alphabetize, and correct your cards as you go along.
- You can block and copy information from your online sources, saving time by not having to write the citation.
- You reduce the number of errors by not writing the same information by hand and then later keyboarding it.
- At the end of the project, you can rework this file to make it into your Works Cited list of sources.

However, be sure to back up your bibliography cards on an external storage system of your choice. In addition, print hard copies as you work. This way, you won't lose your material if your hard drive crashes or the file develops a glitch.

Developing a Working Bibliography

When you start your research, your instructor may ask you to prepare a *working bibliography* listing the sources you plan to use. Your working bibliography differs from your Works Cited page in its scope: your working bibliography is much larger. Your Works Cited page will include only those sources you have actually cited in your paper.

To prepare a working bibliography, arrange your bibliography cards in the order required by your documentation system (such as MLA and APA) and keyboard the entries following the correct form. If you have created your bibliography cards on the computer, you just have to sort them, usually into alphabetical order.

Developing an Annotated Bibliography

Some instructors may ask you to create an *annotated bibliography* as a middle step between your working bibliography and your Works Cited page. An annotated bibliography is the same as a working bibliography except that it includes comments about the sources. These notes enable your instructor to assess your progress. They also help you evaluate your information more easily.

For example, you might note that some sources are difficult to find, hard to read, or especially useful. In Chapter 10, you'll learn how to evaluate your sources—and why it's crucial that you do so.

How Do I Evaluate Sources?

*Nobody outside a baby carriage or a judge's chambers
believes in an unprejudiced point of view.*

—LILLIAN HELLMAN

"All the news that fits we print" might be the unofficial motto
of a free press. One of the great strengths of a free press is its
ability to print anything that does not libel its subject. As far
as researchers are concerned, however, that very freedom presents is own problems. *Just because a source appears in print, in
the media, or online does not mean that it is valid.* As a result, you
must carefully evaluate every source you find before you use it.
This means that you must read critically and carefully.

As you gather your sources, evaluate them carefully.
Three main criteria to use as you determine whether a source
is valid for inclusion in your research paper are quality, bias,
and appropriateness. Let's look at each of these in detail and
then at some special ways to evaluate Internet sources.

Quality

As Spencer Tracey said about Katharine Hepburn in the
movie *Adam's Rib*, "There's not much meat on her, but what
there is is choice." When it comes to movie stars and research
source materials, quality counts.

You want only the choice cuts for your research paper. If
the material isn't of the highest quality, it won't support your

thesis, convince your readers of your point, or stand up under your reader's scrutiny. In fact, it will have just the opposite effect. That's why it's important to evaluate the quality of every source before you decide to include it in your research paper.

The old maxim is true: you *can't* judge a book by its cover. You have to go deeper. Here's how to do it. (Each of the following guidelines holds true for online, print, and media sources.)

- Check the writer's qualifications. Is the writer or speaker *really* qualified to write on the subject? Is this someone you trust to give a valid opinion? You can use the following simple checklist to evaluate the writer or speaker:

  _____ Is the person an expert or an eyewitness to the events described in the source?

  _____ What is the person's reputation?
  You can check in biographical sources such as *Contemporary Biography, Who's Who,* and *Who Was Who* to validate a person's reputation. Web sites often contain biographical information about the various contributors, too.

  _____ Does the person have the credentials to write on this subject?
  Don't be fooled by degrees; a Ph.D. in chemistry, for example, doesn't give a scholar the credentials to write about biology, physics, or any other subject outside his or her field.

  _____ Is the author well known and well respected in the field? How many other online articles, journals, or books has the author published on this subject?

  _____ Does the author have a bias or a personal agenda to advance?
  Is the author selling a product or service, for instance?

- Now, evaluate the source itself. Here are some guidelines to use:

_____ Was the source well reviewed?

Read some critical reviews in quality journals and newspapers to find out how the experts evaluated the publication. If the book was not reviewed, it may not be on the front line of scholarship.

_____ Who spoke in favor of the book?

Most books have endorsements (called "blurbs") penned by well-known people in the field. These usually appear on the back cover of the dust jacket. See whether the endorsements were written by respected writers, scholars, and public figures. If not, the book may not be a solid source.

_____ Is the publisher reputable? Is it known for publishing reliable information?

Reputable sources include scholarly Web sites, scholarly journals, university presses, and major publishers.

_____ Is the source up-to-date? What is the publication date?

_____ Is the source a first edition, revision, or reprint?

While the information in first editions is usually up-to-date, the book may be so new that the information it contains has not yet had time to be authenticated and replicated.

_____ Is the source complete? Have certain facts been cut for their controversial nature or for space limitations?

_____ Does the author present sufficient evidence to support the thesis?

_____ Does the author document his or her claims with the titles, Web sites, and authors of source materials? Are these sources credible?

77

_____ Can the claims in the source be backed up in other sources?

Be especially suspicious of sources that claim to have the "secret" or "inside track." If you can't find the same information in other reputable sources, the material doesn't hold up to scrutiny.

_____ Is the source fair—or does it contain distorted information? The following section shows you how to evaluate sources for bias.

Bias

Every source is biased, because every source has a point of view. Bias is not necessarily bad, as long as you recognize it as such and take it into account as you evaluate and use the source. For example, an article on hunting published in _Field and Stream_ is likely to have a very different slant from an article on the same subject published in _Vegetarian Times_.

Problems arise when the bias isn't recognized or acknowledged. Some problem areas to watch include bogus claims, loaded terms, and misrepresentation.

BOGUS CLAIMS

A claim can be considered _bogus_ or false, when the speaker promises more than he or she can deliver. For example, the speaker may speak vaguely of "many important experiments," or "recent clinical studies" to prove a point. The point may indeed have value, but the studies the speaker cites as proof are too fuzzy to have merit. Well-educated people are rightly skeptical about promises from strangers.

Effective research sources use specific support—not just vague references to unidentified studies and sources. You can't evaluate "many important experiments" or "recent clinical studies" unless you know how they were undertaken, by whom, and where the results were published.

Also be on the lookout for sources that refer to "statistics that show...." Statistics can be very useful in proving a point, but they can also be misleading—especially if you don't have the numbers to evaluate their validity. Ask yourself:

- Does the statistic raise any unanswered questions?
- Has the source of the statistics been revealed?

"Well-known" information is another form a bogus claim can take. Be wary of sources that tell you that "Everybody knows that..." or "It is a well-known fact that...." If the fact is so "well known," why is the writer bothering to cite it as support? Very likely, it's the best support the writer can muster—which doesn't speak well for the validity of the source or writer.

LOADED TERMS

Suspect sources may use "loaded terms" to make their point. A term becomes "loaded" when it is asked to carry more emotional weight than its context can legitimately support. As a result, it becomes *slanted* or *biased*. These sources are often not reliable.

Words with strong *connotations* (emotional responses) often show bias. For example, a writer may refer to the governor's "regime" rather than "administration." "Regime" is a loaded term because it is used to describe oppressive military dictatorships.

While loaded terms are most often used in political writing and speech, they can appear in any source. That's why it's important to read critically.

MISREPRESENTATION

This type of bias takes many forms. First, a writer or speaker can lie outright. Or, a writer may be more subtle, inventing false data or "facts." In addition, dishonest writers often twist what their opponents have said. To misrepresent this way, they use oversimplification. A complex argument can be reduced to ridicule in a slogan or an important element of an argument can be skipped over.

How can you protect yourself from being misled by this type of bias? Here are some issues to consider as you evaluate a text for misrepresentation:

- Is someone quoted out of context?
- Are facts or statistics cited in a vacuum?
- Does the quotation reflect the overall content of the source or does it merely reflect a minor detail?
- Has key information been omitted?

Appropriateness

Even if a source does pass the first two tests and proves to be of high quality and free from bias, it does not necessarily mean that the source belongs to your research paper. For a source to make the final cut, it has to fit with your audience, purpose, and tone. It must be *appropriate* to your paper. How can you decide if a source is suitable for inclusion in your research paper? Try these suggestions:

- Do you understand the material in the source?
- If the source is too technical for you to grasp fully, you might not use it correctly in your paper.
- Is the source written at a level appropriate to your readers?
- Does this source have the information you need?
- Does the source suit your purposes in this research paper?

A Special Note on Evaluating Internet Sources

Be especially careful when you evaluate Web sites because they can be difficult to authenticate and validate. Unlike most print resources such as magazines and journals that go through a filtering process (e.g., editing, peer review), information on the web is mostly unfiltered. What does this mean for you? Here's the scoop: using and citing information found on Web sites is a little like swimming on a beach without a lifeguard.

For instance, Web sites may be published anonymously. This means you can't evaluate the writer or writers. Also, the sites can be updated and revised without notification.

Further, they may vanish without warning. This makes it difficult to evaluate their reliability.

HEADER, BODY, AND FOOTER

Once you've determined that you are dealing with an online source, check the web document for its three main elements: *header, body,* and *footer*. Within each of these pieces, you should be able to determine the following vital elements for evaluating information:

1. **Author or contact person** (usually located in the footer)

   As you evaluate the selection, ask yourself:

   - Who is the author of the piece?
   - Is the author the original creator of the information?
   - Does the author list his or her occupation, years of experience, position, or education?
   - With this information—or lack of it—do you feel this person is qualified to write on the given topic?
   - Where does the online source come from? Knowing the source of a site can help you evaluate its purpose and potential bias.

You can often find clues to the origin of an online source in its address. Look for the suffix to identify the source. Here are the common URL suffixes you'll encounter:

Common URL Suffixes	
Suffix	*Meaning*
com	commercial (business or company)
edu	education (academic site)
gov	government
int	international organization
mil	military organization
net	Internet administration
org	other organizations, including nonprofit, nonacademic, and nongovernmental groups
sci	special knowledge newsgroup

A *.com* is going to have a different slant from a university, for example. It's likely that the .com will want to sell you a product or a service (since it is a business), while the university is probably seeking to disseminate knowledge. As a result, knowing the source of the site can help you evaluate its purpose and potential bias.

2. **Link to local home page** (usually located either in header or footer) and **institution** (usually located in either header or footer).
   As you evaluate the selection, ask yourself:

   - What institution (Like company, government, or university) or Internet provider supports this information?
   - If it is a commercial Internet provider, does the author appear to have any affiliation with a larger institution?
   - If it is an institution, is it a national institution?
   - Does the institution appear to filter the information appearing under its name?
   - Does the author's affiliation with this particular institution appear to bias the information?

3. **Date of creation or revision** (usually located in footer)
   - When was the information created or last updated?

4. **Intended audience** (determined by examining the body)

5. **Purpose of the information**, that is, does it inform, explain, or persuade (determined by examining the body)

6. **Access**, that is, how did you find the site? Was it linked to a reputable site? If you found the site through a search engine, that only means that the site has the words in the topic you are researching prominently placed or used with great frequency. If you found the site by browsing through a subject directory, that may mean only that someone at that site registered it with that directory. If you found it through an advertisement, it is not likely to be reliable.

Given all the information you determined from above, is this piece of information appropriate for your topic? If yes, explain your decision and any reservations you would tell someone else using this information.

ADDITIONAL RESOURCES

Below are some additional links for evaluating web material.

- *Critical Evaluation of Resources.* Margaret Phillips, UC Berkeley Library. Suggestions for evaluating a range of resources, including books, articles, and Web sites. Covers suitability, authority, other indicators, reference sources, and provides links.

- *Evaluate Web Resources.* Detailed checklist under: Introduction, Source, Site/Article, Content, Structure/ Navigation, Links, Site Integrity/Access.

- *Evaluating Credibility of Information on the Internet.* Ronald B. Standler.

- *Evaluating Information found on the Internet.* Elizabeth Kirk, Johns Hopkins University.

- *Evaluating Information: Some questions to help you judge Online Information.* Jacob Hespeler Library.

- *Thinking Critically about World Wide Web Resources.* Esther Grassian, UCLA College Library.

In summary, all sources are *not* equally valid. Be sure to carefully and completely evaluate every source you find before you decide whether to use it in your research paper. Weak or inaccurate sources can seriously damage your credibility as a writer and thinker.

Chapter 11

How Do I Take Notes on My Sources?

One of the skills of research is knowing when you have enough information; in considering too many side issues or too many perspectives, you may lose the main thread of your subject.

—Charles Bazerman

Use sources to help you advance the thesis you have defined. The sources back up your point and help you make new connections among ideas. No matter how many sources you use, their purpose remains the same: to help you make the points you want to make. That's what this chapter is all about.

Reading for Research

Now that you've gathered all your sources (or the vast majority of them), it's time to take notes on the relevant material. "Relevant" is the keyword here. How can you tell what you'll need for your paper and what will end up in the scrap heap?

In most cases you won't be able to tell what's going to make the cut and what won't. As a result, you'll probably end up taking far more notes than you need. Don't worry, nearly all researchers end up with extra notes. The deeper you dig into your subject, however, the more perceptive you'll become about what you need to prove your point most convincingly. Here are some guidelines to help you get started:

- Before you start reading, arrange your sources according to difficulty. Read the general, introductory sources first. Use these to lay the foundation for the more specialized and technical material you'll need.
- Look for facts, expert opinions, explanations, and examples that illustrate ideas.
- Note any controversies swirling around your topic. Pay close attention to both sides of the issue: it's a great way to test the validity of your thesis.
- Read in chunks. Finish an entire paragraph, page, or chapter before you stop to take notes. This will help you get the entire picture so you can pounce on the juicy bits of information.

Taking Notes

No one can remember all the material they read, or keep Expert A's opinion straight from Expert B's opinion. That's why you need to take notes.

For very brief research papers, you can usually gather information without taking notes. In these cases, photocopy the sources, highlight key points, jot ideas in the margins, and start drafting. But with longer, more complex research papers, you'll have to make note cards to handle the flow of information efficiently. Figure on making note cards with any research paper more than a page or two long.

CARD SIZE

Many writers take notes on 4 × 6 index cards. This size is ideal. You don't want cards so small that you can't fit anything on them or cards so large that you'll end up wasting most of the space.

Increasingly, however, writers have been adapting this same method to computer technology. It's very easy to do and can save you a great deal of time when it comes to drafting. Adjust your margins to make a template for a "Notes" file by creating 4 × 6-sized boxes. You can print and cut the cards as you go along. As always, when you are working on a computer, back up all your files on an external storage system. You will also want to print out hard copies as a backup.

OVERALL GUIDELINES

Regardless of how you choose to take notes, the overall techniques remain the same.

- Label each card with a subtopic, in the top right- or left-hand corner.
- Include a reference citation showing the source of the information. Place this in the bottom right- or left-hand corner.
- Be sure to include a page number, if the source is print.
- Write one piece of information per card.
- Keep the note short. If you write too much, you'll be right back where you started—trying to separate the essential information from the nonessential information.
- Be sure to mark direct quotes with quotation marks. This can help you avoid plagiarism later.
- Add any personal comments you think are necessary. This will help you remember how you intend to use the note in your research paper.
- Check and double-check your notes. Be sure you've spelled all names right and copied dates correctly. Check that you've spelled the easy words correctly, too; many errors creep in because writers overlook the obvious words.

Note-Taking Methods

There are three main ways to take notes: direct quotations, summarizing, and paraphrasing. Each is explained below in detail.

TAKING DIRECT QUOTATIONS

A *direct quotation* is word for word; you copy the material exactly as it appears in the source. If there is an error in the source, you even copy that, writing *(sic)* next to the mistake.

Show that a note is a direct quotation by surrounding it by quotation marks ("").

In general, quote briefly when you take notes. Remember that long quotations are difficult to integrate into your paper. Besides, readers often find long quotations hard to follow and boring to read.

What should you quote?

- **Quote key points.** These are passages that sum up the main idea in a pithy way.

- **Quote subtle ideas**. Look for passages whose meaning would be watered down or lost if you summarized or paraphrased them.

- **Quote expert opinions**. They carry weight in your paper and make it persuasive.

- **Quote powerful writing**. If the passage is memorable or famous, it will give your research paper authority.

Example:

Subtopic: Nez Perce surrender

"It is cold, and we have no blankets; the little children are freezing to death. My people, some of them, have run away to the hills, and have no blankets, no food. No one knows where they are—perhaps freezing to death. I want to have time to look for my children, to see how many of them I can find. Maybe I shall find them among the dead. Hear me, my chiefs! I am tired; my heart is sick and sad. From where the sun now stands I will fight no more forever."

Comments: Very moving, emotional speech. Shows tragic consequences of displacement of Native Americans.

Lend Me Your Ears: Great Speeches in History, p. 108

SUMMARIZING

A *summary* is a smaller version of the original, reducing the passage to its essential meaning. Be sure to summarize carefully so you don't distort the meaning of the original passage. What should you summarize?

- Commentaries
- Explanations
- Evaluations
- Background information
- A writer's line of thinking or argument

Example:

Original

"Now, why am I opposed to capital punishment? It is too horrible a thing for the state to undertake. We are told by my friend, 'Oh, the killer does it; why shouldn't the state?' I would hate to live in a state that I didn't think was better than a murderer.

But I told you the real reason. The people of a state kill a man because he killed someone else—that is all—without the slightest logic, without the slightest application to life, simply from anger, nothing else!

I am against it because I believe it is inhuman, because I believe that as the hearts of men have softened they have gradually gotten rid of brutal punishment, because I believe it will only by [be] a few years until it will be banished forever from every civilized country—even New York—because I believe that it has no effect whatever to stop murder."

Summary

Subtopic: Clarence Darrow against capital punishment

Rage and a desire for retribution are not sufficient justification for capital punishment. It is a cruel, inhuman, and uncivilized form of punishment. Further, capital punishment does nothing to deter crime. For these reasons, he believes capital punishment will soon be eliminated, even in New York.

Comments: Original speech has an ironic, sarcastic tone.

Lend Me Your Ears: Great Speeches in History, p. 108

PARAPHRASING

A *paraphrase* is a restatement of the writer's original words. It often includes examples and explanations from the original quotation. A paraphrase may be longer than the original, shorter than the original, or the same length.

Paraphrasing is the most difficult form of note taking. As a result, it is where beginning writers are most likely to commit *plagiarism*—using someone else's words as their own. You can avoid this by quoting words you copy directly and being very sure that you do indeed restate the material in your own words.

You should paraphrase...

- material that readers might otherwise misunderstand.
- information that is important but too long to include in the original form.

Example:
Original
"In the long history of the world, only a few generations have been granted the role of defending freedom in its hour of maximum danger. I do not shrink from that responsibility—I welcome it. I do not believe that any of us would exchange places with any other people or any other generation. The energy, the faith, the devotion which we bring to this endeavor will light our country and all who serve it—and the glow from that fire can truly light the world.

And so, my fellow Americans, ask not what your country can do for you—ask what you can do for your country."

Paraphrase

Topic: Social responsibility (JFK Inauguration speech)

Now, America faces great peril. As a result, America is now faced with the challenge of standing up for liberty. Not many countries have ever been in this position. Kennedy welcomes this challenge because he believes his actions (and America's valiant response) can stand as a beacon for the rest of the world to follow.

"And so, my fellow Americans, ask not what your country can do for you—ask what you can do for your country."

Comments: A very famous and stirring speech.

Lend Me Your Ears: Great Speeches in History, p. 108

Warning!

Don't rely too heavily on any one source—no matter how good it looks. It's fairly common to find one source that seems to say it all, and just the way you like. But if you take too much from one source, you'll end up doing a book report, not a research paper. And worst-case scenario: what happens if the source turns out to be invalid or dated? Your paper will be a disaster.

Now it's time to organize your research into a logical whole. Outlines are the most logical and easy way to accomplish this. Chapter 12 covers everything you need to know to outline your notes.

Part III

Drafting

How Do I Outline—and Why?

A foolish consistency is the hobgoblin of little minds,
Adored by statesman and philosophers and divines.
—RALPH WALDO EMERSON

As this quote indicates, the New England philosopher Ralph Waldo Emerson wasn't overly concerned with being consistent. Where research papers are concerned, however, consistency and order are essential. And there's no better way to show the order of your ideas than with an *outline*. The purpose of an outline is to organize the material you're going to use to prove your thesis. If your information isn't arranged in a logical fashion, your reader won't be able to understand your point.

Why Create an Outline

Some instructors will require you to submit a formal outline with your research paper. These instructors understand that an outline serves as a preview tool that allows them to grasp your thesis and organization at a glance. It explains the scope and direction of your paper as well.

Whether or not you're required to submit an outline with your final paper, making an outline is a superb way to help you construct and classify your ideas. In addition, an outline serves as a final check that your paper is unified and coherent. It helps you see where you need to revise and edit your writing, too.

How to Create an Outline

While outlining is not difficult, it can be challenging to get started. The following suggestions can make the task easier.

1. First, arrange your notes in a logical order that you can follow as you write. If you're having difficulty seeing an order, look for clues in the sequence of your ideas. You can make a diagram, such as a flowchart, to help you visualize the best order to use.

2. Jot down major headings.

3. Sort the material to fit under the headings. Revise the headings, order, or both, as necessary.

4. Look for relationships among ideas and group them as subtopics.

5. Try to avoid long lists of subtopics. Consider combining these into related ideas. In nearly all cases, your paper will be better for having linked related ideas.

6. If you can't decide where to put something, put it in two or more places in the outline. As you write, you can decide which place is the most appropriate.

7. If you're not sure that an idea fits, write yourself a reminder to see where it belongs after you've written your first draft.

8. If an important idea doesn't fit, write a new outline with a place for it. If it's important, it belongs in the paper.

9. Accept your outline as a working draft. Revise and edit as you proceed.

10. After you finish your outline, let it sit for a few days. Then look back at it and see what ideas don't seem to fit, which points need to be expanded, and so on. No matter how carefully you construct your outline, it will inevitably change. Don't be discouraged by these changes; they are part of the writing process.

Form of an Outline

Outlines are written in a specific form, observing specific rules. The following section shows this format.

Model

Thesis statement: Write your thesis statement here.

I. Major topics or paragraphs are indicated by Roman numerals. These are made by using the capitals I, V, or X on your keyboard.
   A. Subheads are indicated by capital letters.
      1. Details are indicated by numbers, followed by a period.
         a. More specific details are indicated with lower-case letters.
         b. These are written a, b, c, and so forth.
      2. Begin each entry with a capital letter.
   B. You can have as many entries as you like, but there must be at least two in each category.
      1. You cannot have a I without a II.
      2. You cannot have an A without a B.
      3. You cannot have a 1 without a 2.
      4. You cannot have a lower case a without a lower case b.
II. Entries should be in parallel order.
   A. Entries may be word entries.
   B. Entries may be phrase entries.
   C. Entries may be sentence entries.

For sample completed outlines, see the model research papers at the end of this guidebook.

Types of Outlines

There are several types of outlines, two of which are discussed below: jotted outlines and working outlines.

JOTTED OUTLINE

A *jotted outline* is a sketch of an outline, a list of the major points you want to cover. A jotted outline is a useful way to organize your thoughts because you can see what you're including at a glance. Here's a model of a jotted outline:

Thesis: Since cigarette smoking creates many problems for the general public, it should be outlawed in all public places.

I. Harms health
   A. Lung disease
   B. Circulatory disease
II. Causes safety problems
   A. Destroys property
   B. Causes fires
III. Sanitation problems
   A. Soils the possessions
   B. Causes unpleasant odors
IV. Conclusion

WORKING OUTLINE

A *working outline,* in contrast, is more fully fleshed out than a jotted outline. Expanded and divided into topics and subtopics, it helps you create a map as you draft your research paper. An effective working outline has the following parts:

1. Introduction
2. Thesis
3. Major topics and subtopics
4. Major transitions
5. Conclusion

Usually, the entries are written as sentences. Here's a model of a working outline, expanded from the previous jotted outline. Note that the entries are written as complete sentences.

Model

Thesis: Since cigarette smoking creates many problems for the general public, it should be outlawed in all public places.

I. Cigarette smoke harms the health of the public.
   A. Cigarette smoke may lead to serious diseases in nonsmokers.
      1. It leads to lung disease.
         a. It causes cancer.
         b. It causes emphysema.

2. It leads to circulatory disease in nonsmokers.
   a. It causes strokes.
   b. It causes heart disease.
B. Cigarette smoke worsens other less serious health conditions.
   1. It aggravates allergies in nonsmokers.
   2. It causes pulmonary infections to become chronic.
   3. It can lead to chronic headache.
II. Cigarette smoking causes safety problems.
   A. Burning ash may destroy property.
   B. Burning cigarettes may cause serious fires.
III. Cigarette smoke leads to sanitation problems.
   A. Ash and tar soil the possessions of others.
   B. Ash and tar cause unpleasant odors and fog the air.
IV. Conclusions
   A. Cigarette smoking injures people's health and so should be banned in all public places.
   B. Cigarette smoking damages property and so should be banned in all public places.

Warning!

In general, a standard high school or college research paper should have no more than four or five main points. This means you shouldn't have more than four or five Roman numerals in your outline. If you have too many ideas, your paper will either be too long or more likely, vague and overly general.

Chapter 13 covers the elements of research paper style to help you craft a research paper that suits your audience, purpose, and topic.

What Writing Style Do I Use?

Wear your learning like your watch, in a private pocket;
do not merely pull it out and strike it; merely to show
you have one.

—LORD CHESTERFIELD

Even if you haven't finished all your research, when you have completed most of your note cards and your outline, it's time to start writing. Drafting at this stage allows you to see what additional information you need so you can fill it in. As you begin to draft your paper, it's time to consider your writing *style*.

Style

A writer's *style* is his or her distinctive way of writing. Style is a series of choices—words, sentence length and structure, figures of speech, punctuation, and so on. The style you select for your research paper depends on the following factors:

- audience
- purpose
- tone

AUDIENCE

Knowing with *whom* you are communicating is fundamental to the success of any message. You need to tailor your writing style to suit the audience's needs, interests, and goals. The audience for your research paper is likely to be one of the following three people or groups:

- your boss, supervisor, professor, teacher, instructor
- your colleagues or classmates
- any outside readers, such as clients

To tailor your research paper to your audience, do an audience analysis. Before you write, ask yourself these questions:

- Who will be reading my research paper?
- How much do my readers know about my topic at this point?
- What is the basis of the information they have? (e.g., reading, personal experience)
- How does my audience feel about this topic? Are they neutral, hostile, enthusiastic, or somewhere in between?
- What style of writing does my audience anticipate and prefer?

PURPOSE

Writers have four main purposes:

- to explain (exposition)
- to convince (persuasion)
- to describe (description)
- to tell a story (narration)

Your purpose in your research paper is to *persuade* or convince. As a result, you'll select the supporting material (such as details, examples, and quotations) that will best accomplish this purpose. As you write, look for the most convincing examples, the most powerful statistics, the most compelling quotations to suit your purpose.

The *tone* of a piece of writing is the writer's attitude toward his or her subject matter. For example, the tone can be angry, bitter, neutral, or formal.

The tone depends on your audience and purpose. Since your research paper is being read by educated professionals and your purpose is to persuade, you will use a formal, unbiased tone. The writing won't condescend to its audience, insult them, or lecture them.

The language used in most academic and professional writing is called "Standard Written English." It's the writing you find in magazines such as *Newsweek, US News and World Report*, and *The New Yorker*. Such language conforms to the widely established rules of grammar, sentence structure, usage, punctuation, and spelling. It has an objective, learned tone. It's the language that you'll use in your research paper.

The Basics of Research Paper Style

The following section covers the basics of research paper writing style.

WORDS

- **Write simply and directly.** Perhaps you were told to use as many multisyllabic words as possible since "big" words dazzle people. Most of the time, however, big words just set up barriers between you and your audience. Instead of using words for the sake of impressing your readers, write simply and directly.

  Select your words carefully to convey your thoughts vividly and precisely. For example, *blissful, blithe, cheerful, contented, ecstatic, joyful,* and *gladdened* all mean "happy"—yet each one conveys a different shade of meaning.

- **Use words that are *accurate, suitable*, and *familiar.***
  - *Accurate* words say what you mean.
  - *Suitable* words convey your tone and fit with the other words in the document.
  - *Familiar* words are easy to read and understand.

As you write your research paper, you want words that express the importance of the subject but aren't stuffy or overblown. Refer to yourself as *I* if you are involved with the subject, but always keep the focus on the subject rather than on yourself. Remember, this is academic writing, not memoir.

- **Avoid slang, regional words, and nonstandard diction**. Below is a brief list of words that are never correct in academic writing. The right-hand column shows the correct words and phrases.

Nonstandard Words and Expressions	
Nonstandard	**Standard**
irregardless	regardless
being that	since
had ought	ought
could of	could have
this here	this
try and do	try to do
off of	off
that there	that

- **Avoid redundant, wordy phrases**. Here are some examples:

Wordy	**Concise**
honest truth	truth
past history	history
fatally killed	killed
revert back	revert
true facts	facts
live and breathe	live
null and void	null (or void)
most unique	unique
cease and desist	cease (or desist)
proceed ahead	proceed

- **Always use *bias-free language.*** Use words and phrases that don't discriminate on the basis of gender, physical condition, age, or race. For instance, avoid using *he* to refer to both men and women. Never use language that denigrates people or excludes one gender. Watch for phrases that suggest women and men behave in stereotypical ways, such as *talkative women.*

  In addition, always try to refer to a group by the term it prefers. Language changes, so stay on the cutting edge. For instance, today the term "Asian" is preferred to "Oriental."

SENTENCES

Effective writing uses sentences of different lengths and types to create variety and interest. Craft your sentences to express your ideas in the best possible way. Here are some guidelines:

- Mix *simple, compound, complex,* and *compound-complex* sentences for a more effective style. When your topic is complicated or full of numbers, use simple sentences to aid understanding. Use longer, more complex sentences to show how ideas are linked together and to avoid repetition.
- Select the subject of each sentence based on what you want to emphasize.
- Add adjectives and adverbs to a sentence (when suitable) for emphasis and variety.
- Repeat keywords or ideas for emphasis.
- Use the active voice, not the passive voice.
- Use transitions to link ideas.

PUNCTUATION

Similarly, successful research papers are free of technical errors. Here are some guidelines to review:

- Remember that a period shows a full separation between ideas.

  Example:
  The car was in the shop for repair on Friday. I had no transportation to work.

- A comma and a coordinating conjunction (*for, and, but, or, yet, so, nor*) show the relationships of addition, choice, consequence, contrast, or cause.

  Example:
  The car was in the shop for repair on Friday, so I had no transportation to work.
  The car was in the shop for repair on Friday, but I still made it to work.
  The car was in the shop for repair on Friday, yet I still made it to work.

- A semicolon shows the second sentence completes the content of the first sentence. The semicolon suggests a link but leaves to the reader to make the connection.

  Example:
  The car was in the shop for repair on Friday; I didn't make it to work.

- A semicolon and a conjunctive adverb (such as *nevertheless and however*) show the relationship between ideas: *addition, consequence, contrast, cause and effect, time, emphasis,* or *addition.*

  Example:
  The car was in the shop for repair on Friday; however, I made it to work anyway.

- Using a period between sentences forces a pause and then stresses the conjunctive adverb.

  Example:
  The car was in the shop for repair on Friday. But I still made it to work.

Warning!
Even if you do run a grammar check, be sure to check and double-check your punctuation and grammar as you draft your research paper.

Writing the Introduction

A research paper, as with any good essay, starts off with an *introduction*. The introduction serves two purposes: it presents your thesis and gets the reader's attention. There are five ways you can do this:

- statement (usually the thesis)
- anecdote (a brief story)
- statistics
- question
- quotation

Select the method that suits your audience, purpose, and tone, as you have learned.

STATEMENT USED AS AN INTRODUCTION

Statement	To Edith Newbold Jones, cross-currents with English influences came early. Unlike other upper-middle-class New York ladies of the 1860s, young Edith grew deeply immersed in her father's impressive library on West
Details	23rd Street. Her reading was mainly concentrated in English authors, for the only American literary works she perused were those of Prescott, Parkman, Longfellow, and Irving. As Louis Auchincloss maintains,
Source material **Lead-in to next** **paragraph**	culture and education, to the Joneses, still meant Europe (Auchincloss, 54). Edith's education bears this out.

ANECDOTE USED AS AN INTRODUCTION

It was the game that could have ended a dynasty. There were only six seconds left on the clock. Seaford was up by one, but they were in trouble on their own 20-yard line without the ball against a powerful Bethpage. It was all up to the kicker to boot the ball through the uprights. The huddle broke and the whistle blew. The

Anecdote —— crowd jumped to their feet, hoping for a miracle. Thump! The ball flew high over the left upright. It didn't look good to the coaches, but the fans went wild. To the coaches' astonishment, the referee in the end zone signaled the kick was good. A look at the videotape told a different story, however. According to the camera, the ball wasn't clear.

Thesis statement —— Instant replay could have changed the outcome of this crucial game—and many others like it on both local and national levels. That's why instant replay should be brought back to the NFL.

STATISTICS USED AS AN INTRODUCTION

Statistics —— According to the National Highway Safety Administration, 1,136 lives have been saved by air bags between the years 1989-1995 and [*www.nhsp.html*]. Since 1991, an increasing number of auto manufacturers have equipped their cars with air bags. As the

Thesis statement —— number of cars equipped with air bags rises, so do the number of lives they save.

QUESTION USED AS AN INTRODUCTION

An allegedly drunk driver runs down a person on a water scooter in the Great South Bay.

A Rocky Point teenager disappeared in rough seas after going fishing in Lake Michigan in a Styrofoam boat lacking a sail, motor, or oars.

A speedboat with four people aboard strikes a rock and capsizes in high winds.

Questions ———	Could these accidents have been avoided if the boat operator had acquired more boating skills? Would mandatory licensing for boat operators help prevent future tragedies? We must have both mandatory safe boating education and licensing.
Thesis ___ **statement**	

QUOTATION USED AS AN INTRODUCTION

Quotation ———	The ads trumpet "You've come a long way, baby" but have we? Nothing could be further from the truth. Today, females have few positive role models, especially when it comes to the media. Television developers and producers have to take a long, hard look at the messages their programs send to the female population and rethink the format of current and future television shows.
Thesis ___ **statement**	

In this chapter, you explored ways to suit your writing style to your audience, purpose, and tone. Now, find out how to use your source material to make your point.

Chapter 14

How Do I Use My Source Material?

You could compile the worst book in the world entirely out of selected passages from the best writers in the world.

—G.K. CHESTERTON

Remember that your purpose in any research paper is to use other people's words and ideas to support your thesis. Since you're not an authority on the subject you're writing about, you *must* rely on recognized experts to help you make your point. How can you smoothly blend source material with your own words? Follow the steps described in this chapter.

Use Cue Words and Phrases

How can you show that the material you are quoting, summarizing, and paraphrasing comes from outside sources and isn't something you made up? It's not enough just to plop the material into your paper, even if you *do* surround any exact quotes with quotation marks.

In addition to the awkwardness this creates, you're sacrificing most of the "punch" carried by expert opinions by not smoothly blending their words in with yours. The reason to use outside sources is to buttress your claims, but if you're not going to give the experts clear credit in your research paper, you are, in effect, wasting their words.

Start by using *cue words* and phrases to set off outside material. As you blend the experts' words, be sure to include

- the source of the material.
- the author's name.
- the author's identity and why the author is important. This tells your readers why they should believe the person you cite.
- the author's credentials, since this lends greater weight to the material.

Examples

In *Shakespeare, The Comedies*, the noted literary critic Kenneth Muir claims that....

In a March 15, 2007 front-page article in the *New York Times*, the well-known consumer activist Ralph Nader stated that...

An October 30, 2007 article on the Harvard University web site reported that Gabriel Corfas, an associate professor of neurology at Harvard Medical School, has uncovered an important signal in brain development that is regulated by a molecule involved in Alzheimer's disease. *http://www.harvard.edu*

Use the specific verb you need to indicate your exact shade of meaning. Below is a selection of verbs you may wish to choose from:

Verbs that Help You Integrate Quotations into Your Text

adds	agrees	argues	concedes
acknowledges	admits	advises	confirms
asks	asserts	believes	concludes
claims	comments	compares	considers
contends	declares	defends	denies
disagrees	disputes	emphasizes	explain
endorses	grants	hints	hopes
finds	holds	illustrates	implies
insists	maintains	notes	observes
points out	rejects	relates	reports
responds	reveals	says	sees
speculates	shows	speculates	states
suggests	thinks	warns	writes

Document the Material

As you include the outside source, be sure to provide enough information so your readers clearly understand where it came from. In most cases, this is done through *parenthetical documentation, footnotes, or endnotes*. These are explained fully in Chapters 16 and 17.

Use the Material to Make Your Point

Never assume that your readers understand why you included a specific piece of information. It may appear that you are simply padding your paper with lots of outside sources. To avoid this misunderstanding and to strengthen your point, point out your message to readers and be sure to make your point. You can do this at the beginning or end of a passage.

Examples

Cue Words	Feminist Gloria Steinem argues that "Employers adhere to a number of beliefs about women that serve to reinforce a pattern of nonemployment
Parenthetical Documentation	and nonparticipation for female employees" (Steinem, 54).
Your Point	Since many employers feel that women work for extra money, women's jobs are nonessential. This leads to the conclusion that men should be hired or promoted rather than women.

Showing the Material Has Been Cut

What happens if a quotation contains material that's irrelevant to your point? You can use an *ellipsis* (three evenly spaced periods) to show that you have omitted part of a quotation.

You can use ellipsis in the middle of a quotation or at the end. Do not use an ellipsis at the beginning of a sentence; just start with the material you wish to quote. If you omit more than one sentence, add a period before the ellipsis to show that the omission occurred at the end of a sentence.

Example

Readers of the *Atlantic Monthly* were astonished to find in the January 1875 issue the debut of one "Mark Twain." The originality of Twain's voice dazzled readers as the *Atlantic* showcased what was to become one of the great passages in American literature: "[Hannibal] the white town drowsing in the sunshine of a summer's morning" is shocked into life by the cry of "S-t-e-a-m-boat a-comin'!" As the Twain critic Justin Kaplan notes, "The gaudy packet ... was Mark Twain's reasserting his arrival and declaring once and for all that his surge of power and spectacle derived not from such streams as the meandering Charles or the sweet Thames but from 'the great Mississippi, the majestic, the magnificent Mississippi, rolling its mile-wide tide along, shining in the sun.'"

> **Warning!**
> Never omit material from a quotation to change its meaning deliberately. This is a sleazy way of slanting a quotation to make it say what you mean. In addition, always be sure that the quotation makes grammatical sense after you have cut it.

Who Gets Credit?

Sometimes you have an idea about your topic but find after researching that you weren't the first person to come up with this idea. To take credit for your original thinking but give credit to others who came up with the idea first, present both versions of the idea and give credit to the outside source. If necessary, explain how your idea is different from the reference you used.

Example
Outside
Source

Since music fans have a great deal of difficulty obtaining tickets for certain concerts, any one customer should be prevented from buying more than four tickets at a time (Harvey, 119). However, this does not prevent scalpers from hiring "ringers" to

Author   *Page number*

Your idea   stand in line and buy blocks of tickets. To overcome this problem, at least one-third of the tickets offered for sale should be set aside for bona fide students.

Setting Off Long Quotations

As mentioned earlier, try to avoid using long quotations in your research paper. But if you must quote more than four typed lines of text, follow these guidelines:

- Indent the quotation one inch from the left margin.
- Do not indent the right margin.
- Do not single-space the quotation; stay with double-spacing.
- Do not enclose the quotation in quotation marks; since it is inset, it is understood to be quoted.

As always, introduce the quotation with a sentence and cue words, usually followed by a colon (:).

Example

In his book *Zen and the Art of Motorcycle Maintenance*, Robert Pirsig extends Twain's idea. As Pirsig explains:

When analytic thought, the knife, is applied to experience, something is always killed in the process. Mark Twain's experience comes to mind, in which, after he had mastered the analytical knowledge needed to pilot the Mississippi River, he discovered the river had lost its beauty. Something is always killed. But what is less noticed in the arts—something is always created too. And instead of just dwelling on what is killed it's important also to see what's created and to see the process as a kind of death-birth continuity that is neither good nor bad, but just *is* (231–232).

Chapter 15

What is Plagiarism—and How Do I Avoid It?

*Borrowed thoughts, like borrowed money, only show
the poverty of the borrower.*
—Marguerite Gardiner

When you use someone else's words or ideas in your research paper, you *must* give credit. Otherwise, you're stealing their work. And whether the theft is intentional or accidental, the effect is the same—failure, humiliation, and perhaps even expulsion. Learn how to avoid literary theft by documenting your sources correctly.

What Is Plagiarism?

Plagiarism is the technical name for using someone else's words without giving adequate credit. Plagiarism is

1. Using someone else's ideas without acknowledging the source.
2. Paraphrasing someone else's argument as your own.
3. Presenting someone else's line of thinking in the development of an idea as if it were your own.
4. Presenting an entire paper or a major part of it developed exactly as someone else's line of thinking.
5. Arranging your ideas exactly as someone else did—even though you acknowledge the source(s) in parentheses.

While plagiarism is a serious lapse in ethics as well as a cause for failure and even expulsion in some schools, documenting your sources correctly is easy. It also gives your research paper authority and credibility. Here's how to do it.

Plagiarism Detection Programs

Thanks to plagiarism detection software such as Turnitin.com and MyDropBox.com, instructors have become even more adept at proving that research papers are plagiarized. These programs quickly and easily show instructors which parts of the research paper the student has copied without attribution. Nearly all high schools, colleges, and universities make this software available to instructors free of charge. This means that it's even easier for an instructor to catch instances of plagiarism—and prove them beyond the shadow of a doubt.

Buying Research Papers

Since instructors first assigned research papers, a handful of dishonest students have devised ways to avoid the onerous task of writing their own. In the old days, students could hire others to write their papers for them or recycle someone else's previously submitted paper. Recently, the Internet has gotten into the act. Some sites offer free research papers; others sell "customized" research papers.

The New York Times recently purchased several of the "customized" papers to evaluate their quality and discovered—to no one's surprise—that they were terrible. Off topic, poorly written, disorganized, and filled with laughable errors, none of the papers would have earned a passing grade, even disregarding the fact that they were completely plagiarized. "If I had paid for this paper," said one instructor involved in the evaluation, "I would have demanded my money back." *The Times* concludes that the sites are a scam, since the customized papers are themselves plagiarized, a series of pasted together parts of other papers lifted off the Web.

How Do I Avoid Plagiarism?

To avoid plagiarism, you should

> Never use someone else's ideas without acknowledging the source.
>
> Never paraphrase someone else's argument as your own.
>
> Never present someone else's line of thinking in the development of an idea as if it were your own.
>
> Never turn in an entire paper or a major part of it developed exactly as someone else's line of thinking.
>
> Never arrange your ideas exactly as someone else did—even though you acknowledge the source(s) in parentheses.

You present original ideas in an original way. You give credit for any research that is not your own.

Ways to avoid plagiarism include always documenting quotations, opinions, and paraphrases and recognizing the difference between fact and common knowledge.

DOCUMENT QUOTATIONS

You must always set off direct quotes with quotation marks and give credit to your original source. It is considered plagiarism if you copy a part of the quotation without using quotation marks—even if you give credit.

Example

Not Plagiarism

In a famous essay on the naturalists, Malcolm Cowley noted, "Naturalism has been defined in two words as *pessimistic determinism* and the definition is true as far as it goes. The naturalists were all determinists in that they believed in the omnipotence of abstract forces." (Becker 56)

Plagiarism

Malcolm Cowley defined Naturalism as "*pessimistic determinism*" and the definition is true as far as it goes. The naturalists were all determinists in that they believed in the omnipotence of abstract forces. (Becker 56)

You must also document the way an author constructs an argument or a line of thinking. In addition, it is considered plagiarism if you try to fob off someone else's opinions as your own.

Examples

Original Source

Probably the most influential novel of the era was *Uncle Tom's Cabin* (1852). More polemic than literature, *Uncle Tom's Cabin* nonetheless provided the North and South with the symbols and arguments they needed to go to war (Levin 125)

Plagiarism

Uncle Tom's Cabin, published in 1852, was likely the most important novel of the pre-Civil War era. Even though the book was more of a debate than a novel, it nevertheless gave the Confederate and Union sides the push they needed to start the Civil War.

Not Plagiarism

As Harold Levin argues in his book *Roots of the Civil War, Uncle Tom's Cabin,* published in 1852, provided America with the impetus it need to plunge into the Civil War. Likely the most important novel of the era, *Uncle Tom's Cabin* cannot be regarded as "literature"—it is too strident for that. Nonetheless, its influence cannot be denied. (125)

DOCUMENT PARAPHRASES

The same holds true for paraphrases. It is not enough just to change a few words. Neither is it enough to rearrange a few sentences. Both practices can result in plagiarism. Study these examples:

Examples

Original Source

William Dean Howells (1837–1920) was the most important literary figure in his time. In addition to championing many American writers such as Edith Wharton and Emily Dickinson, Howells promoted Ivan Turgenev, Leo Tolstoy, Henrik Ibsen, Emile Zola, George Eliot, and Thomas Hardy. (Goldsmith 98)

Plagiarism

William Dean Howells was the top literary person in his time. In addition to advancing the careers of American writers like Edith Wharton and Emily Dickinson, Howells championed the writing of non-Americans such as Ivan Turgenev, Leo Tolstoy, Henrik Ibsen, Emile Zola, George Eliot, and Thomas Hardy.

Not Plagiarism

William Dean Howells was the single most significant editor of his day. Howells helped the careers of Ivan Turgenev, Leo Tolstoy, Henrik Ibsen, Emile Zola, George Eliot, and Thomas Hardy as well as those of Edith Wharton and Emily Dickinson. (Goldsmith 98)

UNDERSTAND THE DIFFERENCE BETWEEN FACTS VS. COMMON KNOWLEDGE

By now you're probably thinking that you have to document every single word in your research paper—or pretty close! Not really. You have to document another person's words, ideas, or argument, and everything that is not *common knowledge*.

It's not difficult to document quotations, opinions, and paraphrases, but differentiating between facts and common knowledge can be tricky. "Common knowledge" is defined as the information an educated person is expected to know. People are expected to know general facts about many categories of common knowledge, including the ones listed below:

art	music	history
geography	literature	films
language	science	social studies
cultural facts	computer science	mathematics

How can you tell if something is common knowledge? If the fact is presented in several sources, odds are good that your readers are expected to know it. This means that you do not have to document it.

Examples of Common Knowledge

- The Civil War started in 1861 and ended in 1865.
- Abraham Lincoln was the president during the Civil War.
- He was assassinated by John Wilkes Booth.
- Andrew Johnson became the new president.

In the following instance, however, the fact is *not* common knowledge and so has to be documented:

121

Examples of Facts Needing Documentation
Original Source
By the time the last canon thundered across the Shenandoah Valley at Antietam, the battlefield echoed with the screams of 20,000 Union and Confederate wounded soldiers. (Harris 415)

Plagiarism
When the last canon roared at Antietam, 20,000 Union and Confederate wounded soldiers were left wounded across the Shenandoah Valley. They were yelling in excruciating pain.

Not Plagiarism
Antietam was one of the most devastating battles of the Civil War. By its conclusion, 20,000 Union and Confederate soldiers were wounded. (Harris 415)

In the following two chapters, you'll learn how to use internal documentation and footnotes/endnotes to document your sources.

Example of Carefully Documented Research Paper

The following research paper was written by Kate Greenberger, a student at George Washington University. As you read, notice how Katie used original information and carefully documented all her sources.

Satan's Sons and Faustus' Friends: The Seductive Face of Evil

Baby, do you understand me now?
Sometimes I feel a little mad
But, don't you know that no one alive can always be an angel
When things go wrong I seem to be bad
'Cause I'm just a soul whose intentions are good
Oh Lord, please don't let me be misunderstood

—"Oh Lord, Please Don't Let Me Be Misunderstood"
by Nina Simone

Considering that Satan, once Lucifer Morningstar, is the most compelling and intriguing character in all of Milton's *Paradise Lost*, it should be little to no surprise to find volumes of literature dedicated to his nature. Is he a hero of the underworld or merely a fool with severe and impossible delusions of grandeur? At least in the beginning of *PL*, Milton paints a Satan of remarkable power and charisma. It is easy to see how one might be tempted to follow him from the glories of Heaven with his intense rhetoric. Yet, as the poem continues, Satan's angelic luster fades away and his physical form turns from angel to demon to cormorant to toad to serpent. Milton clearly intends the reader's opinion of Satan to be confused, combining the foul imagery with emotional speeches that tug at the heartstrings. His misery increases exponentially as the story continues. Those like C.S. Lewis who consider Satan a gross fool do so because his pride carries him to heights that never should be reached. He challenges God Himself for the throne of Heaven, taking a third of the host of angels with him into hell for his insolence. As Satan experiences Paradise for himself, he begins to truly understand what it is he lost when he lost Heaven and his suffering appears to increase, despite having left the tortures of hell. Is he thus a fool for having challenged the might of God or is he hell's own hero for having completed the ultimate revenge against the Creator who cast the rogue angels into hell? There appears to be little challenge between the two terms. He is both the hero and the fool, first the prideful fool, then the triumphant hero, though certainly more the rebellious anti-hero that one sees nowadays than the ideal hero of Arthurian legends and the Crusades.

To take God on in an unholy war is a terrible and misguided idea for anyone. The angel once known as Lucifer completely underestimated his creator and admits as such in the opening of *Paradise Lost*, in which he confesses that "so much the stronger proved He with his thunder; and till then who know the force of those dire arms?" (I.92-94). Even worse, he appears to not have learned his lesson. *Paradise Lost* opens with Satan and his demonic army having just been cast into hell. A battle occurred of epic proportions and Satan's forces lost. One might think that the adversary's mind might be mellowed somewhat by waking up in fire after having lost Heaven forever, but instead one finds that Satan is as ever filled with hatred and pride. "The mind is its own place and in itself can make a Heaven of hell, a hell of

Heaven . . . here we may reign secure, and in my choice to reign is worth ambition though in hell: better to reign in hell than serve in Heaven," (I.254-5, 261–263). Somehow, he has set himself irrevocably on the path to eternal rebellion and damnation, refusing the possibility of repentance and forgiveness. As he approaches Eden in Book 4, he goes beyond setting himself on the path to damnation and foolishly forces himself to deny himself repentance, hollowly uttering words to convince himself that he is through with the light of God forever. "All hope excluded thus, behold, instead of us outcast, exiled, his new delight Mankind created, and for him this world. So farewell hope and, with hope, farewell fear; farewell remorse. All good to me is lost. Evil be thou my good," (IV.105-110). It is clear to the reader that the cherubic Satan does not believe what it is that he is saying. He is creating a mantra for himself to repeat to ease his suffering. And yet, at the same time, he comes to believe it ever so slowly and his angelic luster fades even more as he continues his inspirational monologue. Satan isn't a fool for having challenged God without being fully prepared—though that was a decidedly stupid thing to do—because he was able to throw himself into the fight and come up with ways to get around the gross power imbalance by inventing, using God's own tool of creation against Him. While the rogue angels may not have been prepared or even well balanced against God's angels, they believed in what they were doing wholeheartedly. Satan is continuing the desperate fight against his maker without that crucial belief and that, not the fight itself, is what makes him a fool. C.S. Lewis, according to G. Rostrevor Hamilton in Hero or Fool? lampoons Satan for his convoluted logic post-banishment in Prelude to Paradise Lost. The logic dissolves as Satan becomes more and more emotional as he fiercely fends off his desire for God's presence. Even as the torment of being far from his heart's desire burns within him, he strives to convince himself that the revenge he is committing against God is because he'll never be forgiven and God is a tyrannical leader who deserves the revenge about to be dealt. Satan must talk himself into becoming the devil. Only a fool would ignore the obvious like the adversary does.

And then again, Satan is a leader to his demons. He is their hero and Milton does an excellent job of portraying him as an extremely sympathetic character. In fact, considering Satan is Christianity's physical embodiment of evil, Milton works a miracle to create a Satan that is not only powerful and poignant, but highly persuasive as well. That Milton is able to physically illustrate how deeply seductive evil can be through a poem is frightening. But the Satan of *Paradise Lost* is the hero of hell. When they lie in a lake of fire, all hope of Heaven lost to them, the deadened denizens of hell are aroused by Satan's call to action. It is quite the introduction to the devil. The language is intense and one would readily follow the speaker anywhere one was called. It is then that Satan convinces his followers that it is possible to make a Heaven of their hell simply by the power of belief. The demons manage to do what humans cannot and come to an agreement regarding their best course of action. Satan volunteers himself to undertake the fearsome task at hand. He persuades Sin and Death to open the gates of hell and awkwardly flies through Chaos to face alone God's most beloved creation. As the poem continues, Satan's bravery in battle is revealed. Raphael tells Adam of how the fallen angel felt pain for the first time, yet still clashed swords with the archangel Michael, and how he was undaunted by the new sensation of pain and called upon his doomed forces to create weapons of untold destruction. Throughout the first part of *Paradise Lost*, Satan even maintains a holy glow, though it constantly dims until it disappears. He cuts a massive, beautiful figure as a fallen angel, almost a romantic hero. The most heartbreaking moment of the poem comes as Satan sees Adam and Eve for the first time and realizes who has replaced him. "Not spirits, yet to heavenly spirits bright little inferior, whom my thoughts pursue with wonder, and could love, so lively shines in them divine resemblance..." (IV.361-4). It must be noted that the reason Satan feels such a strong connection to the mother and father of humanity is because of the divinity reflected in their visages. It pains Satan to see the beauty and grace of Adam and Eve because God and all the love He has to offer are woven into every fiber of the lovers. They are a physical embodiment of all that he has lost, surrounded by the lush perfection of Eden and filled with worship and love. And the rising of the love and respect for the new creations is not the act of fool. Hamilton notes, "how Satan's heroic qualities are enhanced by this strain of something approaching tenderness in his character...his courage and willpower are not the expression of a nature irrevocably hardened or incapable of gentle emotion," (25). This is far from the behavior of a fool. Satan has multiple facets to his personality and branding him as merely a fool obliterates that fact. He is the most complicated character in the entire poem, both attractive and pitiful to the reader. A hero, as Andrea Dworkin points out, can be almost anyone. "A man can be a hero because he suffers and despairs; or because he thinks logically and analytically; or because he is 'sensitive;' or because he is cruel. Wealth establishes a man as a hero, and so does poverty. Virtually any circumstance in a man's life will make him a hero to some group of people," (*Quotations...*). Replace "man" with "being" and one can see how Satan is a hero. He had a task to complete: bringing about the Fall of Man. He successfully destroyed the perfection of God's creation, exactly as he intended. One-third of the original host of angels was behind the quest, waiting for their due revenge. After having completed his duty as leader of the rebels, Satan is the hero of the underworld.

It is entirely possible to be a hero and a fool. A being may do incredibly dumb things while blazing in support of a cause. After all, a hero is defined by the American Heritage Dictionary as "a person noted for feats of courage or nobility of purpose, especially one who has risked or sacrificed his or her life," which Satan most certainly has. The nobility of his purpose is entirely in the eyes of the beholder. To those who dwell in hell, there can be no nobler purpose than sticking it to God in the best way possible. In this sense, Satan has proven himself time and time again. Yet, he may appear to be a hero to more than just his fellow demons. His love of divine creation and heart-wrenching denial of Heaven for himself is exactly the kind of emotion that keeps the reader once the great war is over. After the violence, there is love. Hamilton says that "in Satan only is there full knowledge of the terrible conflict on which the human pair enter as novices—that division and union of good and evil which is the very atmosphere of human experience and history," (39-40). Satan cannot possibly be just a fool. Stupid behavior does not make a fool when there is so much heroism and bravery and inner conflict to handle. Satan resonates within the reader because there is something wholly recognizable and familiar about him. He is prideful and deeply torn between powerful internal forces, much like mankind. If man had no pride, there would be no Fall. Satan, more so than any other character in the poem including the members of the Holy Trinity, appears heroic to the impure human nature. He is real in a way Adam and Raphael and Jesus are not. The only other character to come close is Eve in all her flawed glory. Milton knew his audience when he wrote the compelling and entrancing Satan so strong and imperfect. Satan reflects man's own potential for good and evil and pride and heroism and foolishness. The reader can believe in the Satanic hero because it appears so plausible. Satan is more real than God Himself.

Works Cited

The Columbia World of Quotations. New York: Columbia University Press, 1996. www.bartleby.com/66/39/18139.html. 5 April 2005.

Hamilton, G. Rostrevor. *Hero or Fool?* London: George, Allen & Unwin Ltd., 1944.

"Hero." *The American Heritage® Dictionary of the English Language*. 4th ed. 2000.

Milton, John. *Paradise Lost*. Ed. David Scott Kastan. Indianapolis: Hackett Publishing Company, Inc., 2005.

Simone, Nina. "Don't Let Me Be Misunderstood." *Don't Let Me Be Misunderstood*. Polygram, 1989.

Chapter 16

How Do I Use MLA Internal Documentation?

Knowledge is cumulative, and an inherited body of information and understanding is the jumping-off point for the development of more knowledge. We often speak of "standing on the shoulders of giants," that is, of previous generations.

—EARL BABBIE

There are several ways to document your sources. When you are writing in the humanities (such as English, history, and social studies) you most often use the MLA style of *internal documentation,* a method created by the Modern Language Association. (In Chapter 17, you'll learn all about footnotes and endnotes.)

When you use *internal documentation,* you place as much of the citation as necessary within the text. The method makes it easy for your readers to track your sources as they read. Later, they can check your Works Cited page for a complete bibliographic entry. Internal documentation takes the place of traditional footnotes or endnotes.

What should you include in the body of the text? The first time you cite a work in your paper, include as much of the following information as necessary...

- the name of your source
- the writer's full name
- the writer's affiliation page numbers or URLs

Naming the Author—According to Van Wyck Brooks, Twain was a thwarted satirist whose bitterness toward the damned human race was the fruit of a lifelong prostitution of his talents. "The life of a Mississippi pilot had, in some special way, satisfied the instinct of the artist in him.... He felt that, in some way, he had been as a pilot on the right track; and he felt that he had lost this track" (252).

Citing the Source—A recent *Time* magazine article entitled "Video Madness," argues that small children become addicted to video games with devastating results (35).

Omitting the Author or Dealing with an Unknown Author—The Long Island "greenbelt" is becoming seriously damaged by snowmobiles (www.greenbelt.org).

Citing an Indirect Source—Not everyone admired Twain's subjects or style. In a highly influential critical study, Van Wyck Brooks repeated Arnold Bennett's assessment of Twain as a "divine amateur" as well as Henry James' famous comment that Twain appeals to "rudimentary minds" (Brooks 21).

In the next chapter, you'll learn how to use footnotes and endnotes. That is another way to give credit to your sources.

Chapter 17

How Do I Use Footnotes and Endnotes?

They lard their lean books with the fat of others' work.
—ROBERT BURTON

Footnotes and endnotes are another form of documentation used in research papers. Sometimes referred to as the *Chicago Style* or *CMS* (after the University of Chicago's *Manual of Style*), footnotes and endnotes are often used in business, the fine arts, and the sciences to indicate the source of materials the writer incorporated into a research paper.

In this chapter, you'll learn when and how to use footnotes and endnotes.

What Are Footnotes and Endnotes?

A *footnote* is a bibliographic reference indicated by a number in the text. The complete citation is then placed at the bottom ("foot") of the same page. A footnote is normally flagged by a superscript number following that portion of the text the note refers to. Use [1] for the first footnote, [2] for the second footnote, and so on. Continue the numbering throughout the entire paper; do not start new numbers on each page.

[1]First footnote
[2]Second footnote

An *endnote* is identical in form to a footnote. The only difference is the placement: all endnotes are placed at the end of the paper on a separate page labeled "Endnotes."

Never mix both footnotes and endnotes; choose one method or the other.

Examples
The following examples illustrate internal documentation (Modern Language Association (MLA) style) and the use of footnotes (Chicago style).

Internal Documentation
Despite the increasing role of women in the documentation workforce, most women remain in jobs traditionally defined as "women's work." Some employers see women as temporary fixtures in the labor force, predicting they will leave for reasons of marriage or child rearing. These employers tend to shuttle women into jobs where there is little or no room for advancement. (Thompson 65).

Footnote
Despite the increasing role of women in the documentation workforce, most women remain in jobs traditionally defined as "women's work." Some employers see women as temporary fixtures in the labor force, predicting they will leave for reasons of marriage or child rearing. These employers tend to shuttle women into jobs where there is little or no room for advancement.[1]

[1] Roger Eggert, "Women's Economic Equality," *Time* 21 May 2007: 65.

Why Use Footnotes and Endnotes?

Use footnotes/endnotes in your research papers when you

are required to document information without using internal documentation.

want to add observations and comments that do not fit into your text.

Most research papers in the humanities use internal documentation to give credit to sources. However, some instructors prefer footnotes or endnotes to internal documentation. Use the method your audience or instructor prefers.

USING FOOTNOTES/ENDNOTES TO DOCUMENT SOURCES

Examples

Text of Paper

The dramatic increase in women's labor force participation has generated a great deal of public interest, resulting in both social and economic consequences.[1]

Footnote or Endnote

[1]Gregory Brown, *Women and Sex Roles: A Psychological Viewpoint* (New York: Dutton, 2007) 126.

Text of Paper

As the women's movement gained momentum and two-income families became a necessity for attaining middle-class status, polls taken between 1972 and 1997 indicate that the approval of married women working outside the home has steadily increased.[2]

Footnote or Endnote

[2] Chris Siefert, "A Woman's Place is in the House—and Senate. *Ms.* August 2007.

USING FOOTNOTES/ENDNOTES TO ADD OBSERVATIONS AND COMMENTS

Whether you use internal documentation or footnotes/endnotes to give credit to outside sources, footnotes/endnotes are useful for adding commentary, material that your reader will find useful but that doesn't directly pertain to your thesis. The footnote/endnote functions as a parenthetical comment, maintaining the flow of your paper.

Example

Text of Paper

Carlos Baker's biography of *Ernest Hemingway: A Life Story* depicts his subject as a man of great complexity—volcanic, mercurial, frequently tortured.[18]

[18]The Woodrow Wilson Professor of Literature at Princeton University, Baker devoted seven years to the preparation of his acclaimed biography of Hemingway.

Guidelines for Using Footnotes/Endnotes

Method

Choose either endnotes or footnotes. As mentioned earlier, never use both in the same paper. In general, endnotes are easier to use than footnotes.

Numbering

As mentioned earlier, number footnotes or endnotes consecutively from the beginning to the end of your paper. DO NOT assign each source its own number or start with number 1 on each page. Use a new number for each citation even if several numbers refer to the same source.

Placement in the Text

Place each citation number at the end of a direct or indirect quotation in the text.

Footnotes are placed on the bottom of the page on which they appear.

Endnotes are placed on a separate sheet of paper headed *Endnotes* or *Notes* at the end of your research paper.

Format

The numbers are superscript Arabic numerals. This means the numbers are raised a little above the words; many computer programs will do this automatically.

Single-space each footnote, but double-space between entries.

Indenting

Indent the first line of the footnote or endnote the same number of spaces as you did with the other paragraphs in your paper, usually five spaces. The second and all subsequent lines are placed flush left (to the left margin).

Spacing	Leave two spaces after the number at the end of a sentence. Don't leave any extra space before the number.

Footnote and Endnote Format

The format for citing books, periodicals, Internet sources, and other sources differs slightly. Examples of footnote/endnote format for several possible sources are given below.

CITING BOOKS

The basic footnote/endnote citation for a book looks like this:

Footnote number. Author's First Name and Last Name, *Book Title* (Place of publication: Publisher, date of publication), page number.

Examples

Book by one author
[6]Phillip Roth, *Portnoy's Complaint* (New York: Random House, 1969) 231.

Part of a book
[4]David Daiches, "Samuel Richardson," in *Twentieth Century Interpretations of Pamela*, ed. Rosemary Cowler (Englewood Cliffs, New Jersey: Prentice-Hall, 2006) 14.

Encyclopedia
[9]*Funk and Wagnalls*, 12th edition, "New Brunswick."

CITING PERIODICALS

The basic footnote/endnote citation for a magazine, newspaper, or journal looks like this:

Footnote number. Author's First Name and Last Name, "Article Title," *Periodical Title,* date, page number.

Examples

Article in a weekly or monthly magazine
[3]Trish Howard, "Time to Abolish the Electoral College," *Newsweek*, 16 July 2007, 23.

Review of a book, movie, or play
[5]Margaret Singer, "Science Fiction or Science Fact?" Review of *Armageddon* (movie), *The Los Angeles Times*, 11 August 2007, 22A.

Signed newspaper article
[22]Scott Sanders, "E-coli Poses Serious Threat to Travelers," *Washington Post*, 5 March 2007, Early City edition, sec. 3, p. 6.

Unsigned newspaper article
To cite an unsigned newspaper title, begin with the title. Include all information that your reader might need to locate the source, such as the edition, section number or letter, and page number.

"E-coli Poses Serious Threat to Travelers," *Washington Post*, 5 March 2007, Early City edition, sec. 3, p. 6.

CITING GOVERNMENT DOCUMENTS

The basic footnote/endnote citation for a government document looks like this:

Footnote number. Government agency. Subsidiary agency. *Title of Document*. Individual Author, if included. (Publication information, page numbers).

Example
[14]United States Congressional House Subcommittee on Health and Education, *Federal Policies Regarding Distribution of Aid to Dependent Children*. 97th Congress. (Washington, DC: GPO, 2007), 63.

CITING INTERNET SOURCES

It's not as easy to cite Internet sources as it is to cite print sources because standards for citing Internet sources are still being developed. Further, web pages don't have a title page where you can easily locate the information needed for a reference.

Below are two examples of a widely accepted standard format for citing Internet sources. The first date is the date the web page was created or last modified. The second date is the date you accessed the web page. If the web page does not have a modification or creation date, leave it out, but always indicate your access date just before the URL.

[19]Robert Williams, "Community Service as a Requirement for High School Graduation." Area 9 Supervisors, January 2005, 22 April, 2007 <http://www.A9S.gc./lpeas/nsp/1245-09_e.html>.

[19]Emma Steinblock, "Giving Parents the Keys to the Kingdom: Allowing Parents Full Access to their College-Age Children's Grades and Behavior Record." American_Educator, Winter 2004, 2 Nov, 2007 <http://www.americaneducator.org/review/winter2004/steinblock.html>.

CITING LECTURES OR SPEECHES

[13]William T. Greene, "Addressing the Needs of the Learning-Disabled Middle-School Child" (Paper presented at the National Council of Teachers of English 2007 Annual Convention. Detroit: Michigan, 22 November, 2007).

CITING INTERVIEWS

[16]Meish Goldish, personal interview. 31 October 2007.

CITING TELEVISION OR RADIO SHOWS

[6]"AIDS Research," *20/20*. Narr. Barbara Walters, Prod. Kathy Coley, WABC, New York, 14 February, 2007.

Chapter 18

How Do I Create a Works Cited Page?

A research paper is not a list of findings; it is the coherent communication of a meaningful pattern of information.

—RICHARD COE

A *Works Cited* page provides a complete citation for every work you *cited* in your research paper. A *Bibliography* (or *Works Consulted* list), in contrast, provides a full citation for every work you *consulted* as you wrote your paper.

In most academic research papers, instructors require a Works Cited page. However, in business, you may be asked to prepare a Bibliography/Works Consulted list as well. Be sure you know what documentation you are required to submit with your research paper.

MLA Citation Format

Below are the standard MLA (Modern Language Association) citation formats. Remember to use MLA style formatting for papers in the humanities.

CITING INTERNET SOURCES

As you read in Chapter 17, the format for citing an Internet source is still evolving. Below are the minimum requirements as of publication date.

- *Author.* Make every effort to distinguish the author of the content from the page designer and avoid listing the designer as an author. If you can't locate an author citation, begin the reference with the title.

- *Title.* If there is both an individual document title and a publication title, place the publication title after the document title.

- *Date of publication or date of last revision.* If a document includes both a date of creation and a date it was last updated, use only the latter. If no date is included, use the abbreviation n.d. (no date) just as you would for a book or article with no date.

- *URL.* Block and copy the URL to avoid typographical errors.

- *Date that you accessed the page.*

Examples

Internet sources include general web sources, database articles, e-mail, and electronic newsgroups and bulletin boards.

General Web Source

Format
Author. "Document Title." *Publication or Web site title.* Date of publication. Date of access.

Example
Rosenberg, Owen. "Selling Organs for Transplant." *Health Issues Update.* Winter 2005. 10 March 2007 <http//: www.organdebate.org/Winter2005.html>

Database Articles

Cite articles from databases (such as EBSCOhost or Lexis-Nexis) as you would an article from a print journal but include additional information about the electronic source.

Format
Author. "Article Title." *Periodical Title:* volume number (publication date): page numbers (if available). Database name. Database producer. Date of access <URL for database home page>.

Example
Moon, William Least Heat. "Blue Highways." *U.S. News and World Report* (17 January 2005): 12+. 12 May 2007 <http://infotrac. galegroup. com/itweb/athe45935>.

E-mail

To document an e-mail message, provide the following information:

Format
Author's name. "Subject line." Description of message that includes recipient (e.g., *e-mail to the author*). Date of sending.

Example
Lawrence, Charles. "Fair Division." E-mail to Jill Fitzpatrick. 26 May 2007.

Electronic Newsgroups and Bulletin Boards

Format
Include the author's name, the title of the document, the date the source was posted, the medium (online posting), the location online, the name of the network, and the date of access.

Example
Brown, Margery. "Inclusion of Handicapped Children." 20 March 2007. Online posting.ivillage, Children with Special Needs. America Online, 25 March 2007.

CITING BOOKS

The basic citation for a book looks like this:

Format

Author's last name, first name. *Book Title*. Place of publication: publisher, date of publication.

Examples

A book with one author

Hartz, Paula. *Abortion: A Doctor's Perspective, a Woman's Dilemma.* New York: Donald I. Fine, Inc., 1992.

A book with two or more authors

Notice that the first author's name is inverted for alphabetical order.

Example

Landis, Jean M. and Rita J. Simon. *Intelligence: Nature or Nurture?* New York: HarperCollins, 1998.

A book with four or more authors

You can cite all the authors listed or only the first one and then write *et al.* ("and others") for the rest of the authors.

Example

Frieze, Irene H., et al. *Women and Sex Roles: A Psychological Perspective*. New York: W.W. Norton & Company, Inc., 2006.

A corporation

Give the name of the corporation as the author, even if it is the publisher as well.

Example

People for the Ethical Treatment of Animals. *Animal Rights*. New York: PETA, 2005.

An author and an editor

Be sure to include the author's name, the title of the book, and then the editor. Use the abbreviation Ed. whether there is one editor or many.

Example

Nathaniel Hawthorne. *Nathaniel Hawthorne's Tales*. Ed. James Macintosh. New York: W.W. Norton & Company, Inc., 1987.

An editor

Give the name of the editor or editors, followed by *ed.* (if one editor) or *eds.* (if more than one editor).

Example

Ellmann, Richard and Robert O'Clair, eds. *The Norton Anthology of Modern Poetry*. New York: W.W. Norton & Company, Inc., 2005.

A book in a series

After the title, include the name of the series and series number.

Example

Spencer, Evan. *Ernest Hemingway*. Twayne's United States Authors Series 54. Boston: Twayne, 1990.

A translation

After the title, write *Trans.* ("translated by") and the name of the translator.

Example

Voltaire. *Candide or l'optimisme*. Trans. George R. Havens. New York: Holt, Rinehart and Winston, 1969.

First give the name of the author and the title of selection, then the title of the book, the editor, the edition, and the publication information.

Example
Mailer, Norman. "Censorship and Literary Cowardice." *Lend Me Your Ears: Great Speeches in History.* Ed. William Safire. New York: W.W. Norton & Company Inc., 1992.

CITING PERIODICALS
The basic citation for an article looks like this:

Format
Author's last name, first name. "Title of the Article." *Magazine.* Month and year of publication: page numbers.

A note on numbers...
- If the page numbers in an article are not consecutive, cite the first page number followed by a plus sign (+).
- The date in a bibliographic citation is written in European style, with the date *before* the month, rather than *after*. For example: 12 September 1989

Examples
Article in a monthly magazine
Crowley, J.E., T.E. Levitan and R.P. Quinn. "Seven Deadly Half-Truths About Women." *Psychology Today* March 1978: 94–106.

Article in a weekly magazine
Schwartz, Felice N. "Management, Women, and the New Facts of Life." *Newsweek* 20 July 2006: 21–22.

Signed newspaper article
Ferraro, Susan. "In-law and Order: Finding Relative Calm." The *Daily News* 30 June 1998: 73.

Unsigned newspaper article
"Beanie Babies May Be a Rotten Nest Egg." *Chicago Tribune* 21 June 2004: 12.

Editorial
Show that the article is an editorial by writing *Editorial* after the title.

Example
"Dealing with the National Debt." Editorial. *Newsday* 12 October 2007, sec. 2:4.

Review
To indicate that an article is a book, movie, or play review, write "Rev. of" before the work being reviewed. Use the abbreviation "dir." for the director.

Example
Barnes, Clive. "The Story of a Life." Rev. of *Collected Stories*, dir. Liz Uslan. The *New York Times* 1 August 2006: 34–35.

CITING PAMPHLETS

Cite a pamphlet the same way you would a book.

Example

Jaffe, Natalie. "Men's Jobs for Women: Toward Occupational Equality." *Public Affairs Pamphlet* 606 (August 1968): 10–17.

CITING GOVERNMENT DOCUMENTS

The format varies with the information available. The basic citation for a government document looks like this:

Format

Government agency. Subsidiary agency. *Title of Document.* Publication information.

Examples

U.S. Department of Labor Statistics, 2007.

United States Congressional House Subcommittee on Health and Education. Federal Policies Regarding Distribution of Aid to Dependent Children. 97th Congress. Washington, DC: GPO, 2007.

CITING LECTURES OR SPEECHES

Format

Name the speaker, the title of the speech, the name of the occasion or sponsoring organization, the location, and the date. If you can't get all this information, provide as much as possible.

144

Sorenson, Sharon. "Addressing the Needs of the Learning-Disabled Middle-School Child." National Council of Teachers of English Annual Convention. Detroit: Michigan, 22 November, 1998.

CITING INTERVIEWS

Format

Subject of the interview. *Personal interview* or *Telephone interview*. Date.

Example

Goldish, Meish. Personal interview. October 31 2007.

CITING TELEVISION OR RADIO SHOWS
Format

Significant people involved with the production. Their role: Writ. (writer), Dir. (director), Perf. (performer), Narr. (narrator), Prod. (producer).

Example

"Universal Health Care." *20/20*. Narr. Barbara Walters. Prod. Sammi Rosen. WABC, New York, 14 February 2007.

Page Format

The Works Cited page (or the Bibliography) is the last page of your paper. Here are some additional guidelines to follow as you prepare this page:

- **Title.** Center the title Works Cited on the top of the page, about one inch from the top. Do not underline it, boldface it, or place it in italics.
- **Alphabetical order.** Entries are arranged in alphabetical order according to the author's last name. If the entry doesn't have an author (such as an encyclopedia entry or an editorial), alphabetize it according to the first word of the title. Ignore the prepositions *A, An*, and *The*.
- **Numbering.** Do not number the entries.

- **Indentation.** Start each entry flush left. Don't indent the first line, but do indent the second and all subsequent lines of an entry. Use the standard indent of five spaces.
- **Spacing.** As with the rest of your paper, double-space each entry on your Works Cited page.

In the next chapter, you'll learn how to present your research paper.

Chapter 19

How Do I Present My Research Paper?

The ink of the scholar is more sacred than the blood of the martyr.

—Muhammad

You're in the home stretch! Just a few more matters to attend to and you'll be ready to hand in your research paper. Now it's time to consider the material that comes before the body of your paper (the *front matter*) and the material that comes after (the *end matter*). It's also time to learn how to present your paper, including typing and binding.

Front Matter

Depending on the subject matter of your research paper and the course requirements, you may need to include specific material before the body of your paper. This includes:

- Title page
- Table of contents
- Foreword
- Preface
- Abstract

147

Always check with whomever requested the research paper (college instructor, work supervisor, and so on) to see if you are required to include front matter and, if so, which elements are required.

TITLE PAGE

Most high school and college research papers require a title page. Your title page should contain:

- the title
- your name
- the name of the course
- your instructor's name
- the date

Here's how to arrange the information:

- *Title.* Center your title one-third down the page. (Repeat the title on the first page, centered on the first line. Double space between the title and the first line of the text.)
- *Your Name.* Place your name halfway down the page, prefaced by the word "by."
- *Course name, instructor's name, date.* These go directly under your name. Double-space between lines.

If your instructor does not require a title page, your first page functions as a title page.

TABLE OF CONTENTS

The *table of contents* lists the main divisions of your paper. If you include a table of contents, be sure that the headings on the table of contents match the headings in each section of your paper. The table of contents appears directly after the title page. Type it up last so you will know the page numbers.

FOREWORD AND PREFACE

It is unusual to include a foreword or preface in a high school or college research paper.

- In most cases, the *foreword* is written by an expert in the field and serves as an endorsement of the contents.
- The *preface,* written by the author of the paper, explains how the paper came to be written and gives thanks to people who helped with research and other related matters.

ABSTRACT

An *abstract* is a brief summary of the contents of your paper. Objective in tone, abstracts are often included in technical or scholarly papers. An abstract usually runs between 100–125 words. It is presented on a separate page in one paragraph. Do not indent the first line.

Example

Abstract

How the Division within the Liberal Community was Reflected in the Nation, 1930–1950

Granville Hicks charged in the New Masses in 1937 that the *Nation* had abandoned its long-held position as unofficial organ of the Liberal Left when it deliberately selected anti-Stalinist reviewers for books dealing with Soviet Russia. The *Nation* called the charges unjustified. Fourteen years later, Hicks once again attacked the *Nation*, this time charging that the editorial section gave the Russians the benefit of every doubt.

Hicks was correct in his charges and in this seesaw of beliefs and allegiances lies the main story of our time. The initial pull of Communism, drawing away, and resulting break-up of the Left determined the literary course of American radicalism.

End Matter

End matter may include visuals, such as charts and graphs, and a glossary.

VISUALS

Visuals include graphs, charts, maps, figures, and photographs. You can draw them by hand or prepare them on a computer. Place each graphic at the appropriate place in the text or group them at the end.

GLOSSARY

A *glossary* lists and defines technical terms or presents
additional information on the subject. For example, if you
are writing a research paper on Shakespeare, you might
include a brief glossary of Shakespearean English, a glossary
of films that tie in with the topic, or a glossary of notable
Shakespearean actors or performances.

Presentation Format

Research papers follow a standard presentation format. They
are *never* submitted in handwritten form. If you have a situation
that prevents you from keyboarding your paper, be sure to
speak to your instructor well in advance of the paper's due date.
Follow these guidelines:

Paper stock   Use white paper, standard $8^1/_2 \times 11''$ size.

Fonts   Use standard 12-point fonts such as Times
Roman, Courier, or Helvetica. Avoid fancy,
elaborate fonts, since they are difficult to
read.

Spacing   Double-space the text. Leave a $1^1/_2''$ margin on the left side and 1" on the other
sides. Your computer is preset for the correct margins.

Justification   Do not right-justify (align) your paper. The
right margins should be ragged. Your com-
puter will automatically justify your left
margin.

Pagination   Number each page and write your name on
the upper-right-hand corner. Do not place
a number on the title page, but count it in

	the final number of pages you submit. Your computer software program creates an automatic page header. This inserts your name and the page number automatically on each page.
Indenting	Indent five spaces at the beginning of each paragraph. Do not skip lines between paragraphs.
Order of pages	Arrange your pages in this order: Title page (if required) Outline (if required) The body of the paper Any relevant end matter Works Cited
Binding	Check with your instructor for specific guidelines. Some instructors require research papers be presented in folders; others discourage this.

Additional Guidelines

Every scholarly field has a preferred style of presentation. Here are some of the standard style manuals for different fields.

- **Biology.** Council of Biology Editors. *Scientific Style and Format: The CBE Manual for Authors, Editors, and Publishers*, 6th edition. New York: Cambridge University Press, latest edition.

- **Chemistry.** American Chemical Society. *The SCS Style Guide: A Manual for Authors and Editors*. Washington: ACS, latest edition.

- **English and the Humanities.** Gibaldi, Joseph. *MLA Handbook for Writers of Research Papers*. 4th edition. New York: Modern Language Association, latest edition.

- **Engineering.** Michaelson, Herbert B. *How to Write and Publish Engineering Papers and Reports*. 3rd Edition. Phoenix, Arizona: Oryx, latest edition.

- **Geology.** United States Geological Survey. *Suggestions to Authors of the Reports of the United States Geological Survey.* 7th ed. Washington: GPO, latest edition.
- **Law.** The Bluebook. *A Uniform System of Citation.* Comp. Editors of Columbia Law Review et al. 15th ed. Cambridge: Harvard Law Review, latest edition.
- **Linguistics.** Linguistic Society of America. *LSA Bulletin,* Dec. issue, annually.
- **Mathematics.** American Mathematical Society. *A Manual for Authors of Mathematical Papers.* 8th Rev. ed. Providence: AMS, latest edition.
- **Medicine.** Iverson, Cheryl, et al. *American Medical Association Manual of Style.* 8th ed. Baltimore: Williams, latest edition.
- **Music.** Holoman, D. Kern, ed. *Writing About Music: A Style Sheet from the Editors of 19ᵗʰ Century Music.* Berkeley: University of California Press, latest edition.
- **Physics.** American Institute of Physics. *AIP Style Manual.* 4th ed. New York: AIP, latest edition.
- **Psychology.** American Psychological Association. *Publication Manual of the American Psychological Association.* 4th ed. Washington: APA, latest edition.

Part IV

Writing the Final Copy

Chapter 20

How Do I Revise, Edit, and Proofread?

The difference between the right word and the nearly right word is the same as that between lightning and the lightning bug.

—MARK TWAIN

Revising

When you think "revising," think "rewriting." Your first draft will rarely say all that you want to say in the best possible way. Experienced writers know that it takes several drafts to convey your meaning clearly. This is especially true when you're writing a research paper, where outside material is used to support your thesis.

Here are some guidelines to follow as you revise your research paper:

- Give your writing time to sit and "cool off" between drafts. Problems often become much clearer if you let some time elapse between writing and revision.
- Allow sufficient time for revision. It's not unusual to spend as much time—if not more—revising than writing.
- Don't be afraid to make significant changes as you revise. You will most likely change the order of paragraphs, delete sections, and add new passages, for instance.

- Save successive drafts of your documents in different computer files, such as researchpaperversion1.doc, researchpaperversion2.doc, researchpaperversion3.doc, and so on. You might find a use for deleted material later.
- Share your writing with others. Peer reviewers can often help you spot areas that need revision. Consider their comments carefully.
- If your school or university has a Writing Center, have them help revise your paper, too.

Editing

Use the following checklist as you edit your paper:

_____ Is my writing *accurate*?

_____ Are my sentences *concise* and to the point?

_____ Have I included sufficient *detail*? Does my paper have all the information and explanation I need to support the thesis?

_____ Do I *prove my thesis*?

_____ Do I use the level of *diction* appropriate for my audience?

_____ Is my writing *coherent*? Do I link related ideas with transitions?

_____ Does my writing have a clear *voice?* Is the voice appropriate to the subject and audience?

_____ Have I *given credit* to each source? Have I avoided plagiarism?

_____ Is my paper in the correct *form*, including a title page, outline, Works Cited page, and anything else required by the assignment?

_____ Is my writing *correct?* Have I used the correct grammar, spelling, and punctuation?

Proofreading

As you prepare your final draft, proofread it carefully to catch any typos or other errors. Read your draft aloud, very slowly, saying each word. Use a ruler or piece of paper to guide your eyes to make sure you don't skip any words. It's also helpful to ask one or more people to proofread your paper as well.

CORRECTING MISUSED WORDS

Too many errors in spelling, punctuation, and grammar can harm an otherwise competent research paper and seriously affect your grade. If you are writing for business, the repercussions can be even more serious.

Spell checkers are very useful inventions, but they have several shortcomings. As a result, you must proofread your paper carefully to catch misused words. This is crucial because it helps you write exactly what you mean. Often people use the wrong word, a common problem with *homonyms* and *homophones*, words often confused.

Homonyms are words with the same spelling and pronunciation but different meanings.

> **Examples: *beam* (ray of light) and *beam* (girder).**
> Homophones are words with the same pronunciation but different spellings and meanings.

> **Examples: *course* (route), *course* (program of study), and *coarse* (rough).**
> English has many of these often-confused words. Use the following list as a guide as you edit and revise your research paper.

THE 60 MOST OFTEN CONFUSED WORD GROUPS

1. *accept:* take
   except: leave out, to exclude
2. *advise:* give counsel
   advice: counsel
3. *air:* atmosphere
   err: make a mistake

4. *affect:* influence (verb)

   affect: a particular psychological state (noun)

   effect: impact and purpose (noun)

   effect: bring about (verb)

5. *a lot:* many

   allot: divide

6. *altar*: a platform upon which religious rites are performed

   alter: change

7. *allowed*: given permission

   aloud: out loud, verbally

8. *all together*: all at one time

   altogether: completely

9. *allude:* refer to

   elude: escape

10. *already:* previously

    all ready: completely prepared

11. *allusion:* a reference to a well-known place, event, person, work of art, or other work of literature

    illusion: a misleading appearance or a deception

12. *among:* three or more people, places, or things

    between: two people, places, or things

13. *amount:* things that *can't* be counted (example: *amount* of sunlight)

    number: things that *can* be counted (example: *number* of bricks)

14. *arc:* part of the circumference of a circle; curved line

    ark: boat

15. *are:* plural verb

    our: belonging to us

16. *ascent:* move up

    assent: agree

17. *bare:* undressed

    bare: unadorned, plain

bear: large wild animal

bear: carry, hold

18. *base*: the bottom part of an object; the plate in baseball; morally low

    bass: the lowest male voice; a type of fish; a musical instrument

19. *beau*: sweetheart

    bow: bend from the waist; a device used to propel arrows; loops of ribbon; the forward end of a ship

20. *berth*: a sleeping area in a ship

    birth: being born

21. *board*: a thin piece of wood; a group of directors

    bored: not interested

22. *born*: native, brought forth by birth

    borne: endured (past participle of "to bear")

23. *bore*: tiresome person

    boar: male pig

24. *brake*: a device for slowing a vehicle

    break: crack or destroy

25. *bread*: baked goods

    bred: cause to be born

26. *breadth*: the side-to-side dimension

    breath: inhalation and exhalation

27. *bridal*: pertaining to the bride or a wedding

    bridle: part of a horse's harness

28. *buy*: purchase

    by: near or next to

29. *capital*: the city or town that is the official seat of government; highly important; net worth of a business

    Capitol: the building in Washington D.C. where the U.S. Congress meets

30. *conscience*: moral sense

    conscious: awake

31. *cell*: a small room, as in a convent or a prison
     sell: trade
32. *cent:* a penny
     scent: aroma
33. *cheep:* what a bird says
     cheap: not expensive
34. *deer*: animal
     dear: beloved
35. *do*: act or make (verb)
     due: caused by (adjective)
36. *draft*: breeze
     draft: sketch
37. *dye*: change color
     died: ceased living
38. *emigrate:* move away from one's country
     immigrate: move to another country
39. *eminent:* distinguished
     imminent: expected momentarily
     immanent: inborn, inherent
40. *fare*: price charged for transporting a passenger
     fair: not biased; moderately large; moderately good
41. *faze*: stun
     phase: a stage in someone's behavior
42. *for*: because
     four: the number 4
43. *gorilla*: ape
     guerrilla: soldier
44. *grate*: irritate, reduce to small pieces
     great: big, wonderful
45. *hair*: the stuff on your head
     heir: beneficiary of a deceased person's estate
     hare: rabbit like animal

46. *here*: in this place
    hear: listen
47. *hours*: 60-minute period
    ours: belonging to us
48. *it's*: contraction for "it is"
    its: possessive pronoun
49. *lay*: to put down
    lie: be flat
50. *lead*: conduct
    lead: bluish-gray metal
    led: past tense of "to lead"
51. *loose*: not tight, not fastened (noun)
    loose: untighten or let go (verb)
    lose: misplace (verb)
52. *meat*: animal flesh
    meet: encounter; proper
53. *peace*: calm
    piece: section
54. *plain*: not beautiful; obvious; also, a flat stretch of land
    plane: airplane; in geometry, a two-dimensional surface
55. *presence*: company, closeness
    presents: gifts
56. *principal*: main; head of a school
    principle: rule
57. *reed*: plants
    read: interpret the written word
58. *right*: correct
    write: form letters
59. *than*: comparison
    then: at that time
60. *their*: belonging to them
    they're: contraction for "they are"
    there: place

Learning some standard spelling rules can serve you well as you proofread your research papers. Here are the basics:

1. **i before *e* except after *c*. . .**

   i before e except after c

   or as sounded as a as in *neighbor* and *weigh*

   ### Examples: Words That Fit the Rule

i before e	*except after c*	*sounded as a*
achieve	conceit	neighbor
believe	ceiling	weigh
siege	receive	freight
relief	conceive	reign
grief	deceit	sleigh
chief	deceive	vein
fierce	perceive	weight
fiend	receipt	beige
piece	receive	eight
shriek		feint
bier		heir
yield		surveillance
relieve		veil
piece		

   ### Examples: Words That Don't Fit the Rule

either	neither	foreign	height
leisure	seize	weird	protein
codeine	financier	glacier	counterfeit
Fahrenheit	fiery		

2. ***e, i, e, i (no o).*** Words with *i* and *e* pronounced with a long *a* sound are always spelled *-ei*, never *-ie*.

   ### Examples

eight	feign	sleigh
vein	neigh	peignoir

   If the sound is a long-*i,* the word is usually spelled with the *-ei* combo, not *-ie.*

   ### Examples

feisty	stein	seismic
height	leitmotif	

Notice that in each case, the -ie combination is followed by an *r*.

In addition, "*ie*" words with a short vowel sound usually spell it -*ie* rather than -*ei*.

Examples

patient	friend	transient
sieve	mischief	handkerchief

Common Exceptions

heifer	nonpareil	sovereign
counterfeit	surfeit	

3. **The -*ceed*/-*cede* rule.** There are only three verbs in English that end in -*ceed*: *succeed, proceed, exceed.* All the other verbs with that sound end in -*cede*. For example, *secede, recede, intercede, concede, accede, cede, precede.*

4. **The -*ful* rule.** Remember that the sound *full* at the end of a word is spelled with only one *l*.

Examples

Root Word	+	Suffix	=	New Word
care	+	ful	=	careful
grace	+	ful	=	graceful
hope	+	ful	=	hopeful

When the suffix is -*ful* plus -*ly*, there are two l's.

Examples

Root Word	+	Suffix	=	New Word
restful	+	ly	=	restfully
thankful	+	ly	=	thankfully
zestful	+	ly	=	zestfully

5. **-*ery* or -*ary*?** Only six commonplace words end with -*ery* as opposed to -*ary*. They are: *cemetery, confectionery, millinery, monastery, distillery, stationery (writing paper).*

6. **Q is followed by u.** This is a nice rule because it has only one English exception, the lightweight nylon fabric called *Qiana.* The rule doesn't fit with abbreviations or foreign words, however. For instance, the abbreviation for

quart is *qt.* (not *qut.*) The east Arabia peninsula on the Persian Gulf is *Qatar*, not *Quatar*, but that's ok, because the word can also be spelled "Katar."

7. **ks and cs.** Some words that end in c have a hard "k" sound. Adding *y, i,* or *e* after the final c changes the hard sound to a soft one, creating spelling dilemmas. As a general rule, add a *k* after the final *c* when the hard sound becomes soft.

Examples

Word ending in C	Adding the K
mimic	mimicked, mimicking, mimicker
traffic	trafficked, trafficking, trafficker
panic	panicked, panicking, panicky

8. **Compound words.** Compound words fall into three categories: *open compounds, closed compounds, hyphenated compounds.* Here are the definitions and examples:

Open compounds are written as two words:
cedar shingles   night shift   executive secretary

Closed compounds are written as one word:
handbook   northeast   homemaker

Hyphenated compounds have a hyphen:
president-elect   over-the-counter

Warning!

A *hyphen* is one press of the button -; a *dash* is two—. A hyphen is used *within* words; a dash is used *between* words.

PROOFREADING SYMBOLS

What happens if you have completely finished proofreading your paper and you suddenly spot a few more errors? Don't panic. If there are only a few errors, use the following proofreading marks rather than retype an entire page.

Proofreading Marks

Lowercase	*lc*	Period	⊙
Capital letter	*cap or*	Comma	⋀
Close up space	⌗ *or* ⌒	Colon	⊙
Insert space	∧⌗	Semicolon	⋀
Paragraph	¶	Question mark	**?**
No paragraph	*no* ¶	Apostrophe	⋁
Delete	ℓ	Open quotes	⋎
Delete and leave one space	ℓ *or* ⌗ℓ	Close quotes	⋎
Delete and close up	ℓ	Hyphen	|=|
Let it stand	(*stet*)	Dash	$\frac{1}{N,}$ $\frac{1}{N,}$ $\frac{2}{N,}$ $\frac{3}{N}$
Flush left, right	[ ]	Parentheses	⧸ ⧹
Brackets	⧸ ⧹	Move right or left	⟵ ⟶
Center	] [	Transpose	∿
Align horizontally	⑂	Insert letter	∧
Align vertically	≋	Underscore	*u.s.*
Boldface	∿∿∿∿∿	Italic	_____

Chapter 21

Model Papers

Use the following research papers as guidelines as you prepare your own.

Model #1: Prozac and Other SSRIs: Salvation or Damnation?

Thesis: SSRIs should be used with great care.

I. Introduction
   A. Anecdotal opening
   B. Thesis
II. Background
   A. How SSRIs works
   B. Statistics on sale and use
III. Advantages of SSRIs (opposition side)
   A. Emotional calm
   B. Fewer side effects than other antidepressants
   C. Helps many patients
IV. Disadvantages of SSRIs (writer's side)
   A. Side effects may outweigh advantages
      1. Thoughts of suicide
      2. Emotional void
      3. Decreased libido
      4. Personality changes
      5. May accelerate tumor growth
      6. Other side effects
   B. May be overprescribed.
   C. Provides only a quick-fix
V. Conclusion

Prozac and Other SSRIs: Salvation or Damnation?

Melissa Ryder was suffering from depression. To
relieve her symptoms, her doctor prescribed Prozac.
"After only six days on Prozac, I was in far worse
shape than I had ever been before," she said in an
interview. Her bizarre side effects included dreams
of bouncing off walls, uncontrollable trembling,
urges to stab herself, and thoughts of killing her
children. Melissa Ryder is no longer using Prozac
and her condition has improved greatly (Bowe 42).

Despite the tremendous global popularity of
Prozac and other drugs classified as selective
serotonin reuptake inhibitors (SSRIs), some serious
issues are being raised about their negative
effects. The side effects of SSRIs can do more damage than the makers of the drugs could have ever
imagined, as Melissa Ryder's case illustrates.
While SSRIs can help some people suffering from
depression and other mental disorders, they should
only be used with great care.

Prozac, also known by its chemical name
Fluoxtine, is the first "designer drug" created
expressly to treat depression by altering the bio-
chemistry of only one system in the brain. Prozac
interferes with the reabsorption process of serotonin going into the brain. It slows down the
uptake of serotonin, making it more available to
the brain when needed (Brown 153).

Prozac and related SSRIs have been one of modern medicine's great success stories. In an article
entitled "Trouble in Prozac" in *Fortune* magazine,
writer David Stipp notes that since Prozac's debut

in 1988, the drug has grown into an $11-billion-a-year market in the U.S. alone. Nearly 150 million U.S. prescriptions were dispensed in 2004 for SSRIs and similar antidepressants called SNRIs, according to IMS Health, a Fairfield, Connecticut drug data and consulting company—more than for any other drug except codeine. Approximately one out of every twenty adult Americans take SSRIs now, making brands like Pfizer's Zoloft, GlaxoSmithKline's Paxil, Forest Laboratories' Celexa, and Solvay Pharmaceuticals' Luvox household names. These figures show that Prozac and related SSRIs must be helping many people. <http://money.cnn.com/magazines/fortune/fortune_archive/2005/11/28/8361973/index.htm>

These drugs clearly have some advantages in the treatment of depression. Doctors boast that SSRIs afford some patients a consistent, calm feeling, unlike that achieved through other antidepressants that have less severe side effects than SSRIs. According to science writer Claudia Bowe, "SSRIs happens to have fewer side effects because they alter one brain chemical (serotonin), while most other anti-depressants affect many chemical systems in the brain" (44)

Describing her depression, Margaret London, an office manager in Manhattan, said, "Everything was gray and black. It was like being in a pit." Ms. London tried all the different kinds of anti-depressants currently on the market, but only Prozac helped her. She said, "After being on Prozac, I began to realize that I no longer felt depressed and unhappy. I felt as if someone had whitewashed the world" (Bowe 42).

Although Prozac was beneficial to Margaret London, for many patients, the side effects of SSRIs greatly outweigh their benefits. The negative effects of SSRIs range from suicide to sexual dysfunction. Martin Teicher, a psychiatrist from Boston University, studied his patients on Prozac and concluded, "A significant percentage of Prozac users were thinking of stabbing themselves, turning on gas jets in their apartments and striking a match to blow themselves up" ("Open Verdict" 76). Other psychiatrists have reported similar results. In 2005, Tim "Woody" Witczak killed himself at age 37, soon after going on Zoloft, the top-selling member of Prozac's class of drugs. Her husband was an upbeat, happy man, says Kim Witczak, but he had been prescribed Zoloft for insomnia over a new job. Soon after he started taking the drug, Witczak began suffering from nightmares, profound agitation, and eerie sensory experiences. Five weeks after his first dose, he hanged himself. Witczak's death is not an isolated incident. Similar cases date back more than a decade. In September 1989, for instance, a man taking Prozac shot twenty people and then killed himself. His doctor said that the man was not violent until he began taking Prozac. As a result of this incident, lawsuits amounting to hundreds of millions of dollars have been filed against Eli Lilly, the company that sells Prozac ("Open Verdict" 76).

There are also complaints of people feeling devoid of emotions while on Prozac. Dr. Randolph Catlin, a psychiatrist and chief of the mental health service at Harvard University, said, "Many of the students I treated with Prozac reported split off from themselves. They felt as though they were not there anymore." He added, "One wonders if these reports that you hear about patients acting aggressively while on Prozac might be cases where patients who are out of touch with their feelings act on their impulses, without having any feelings of guilt or concern" (Nichols 39).

Dulled or absent sexual response is a problem, too. It has been reported that some individuals on Prozac have a decreased libido or no desire for sexual activity. A U.S. study, published in *The Journal of Clinical Psychiatry* in April 1994, found that among 160 patients taking Prozac, 85 reported that their sexual desire or response diminished after using Prozac (Nichols 36).

In addition, many patients on Prozac began to experience personality changes over time. A new study described at the annual meeting of the American Psychiatric Association suggests that Prozac alters aspects of personality as it relieves depression. Ron G. Goldman a psychiatrist at Columbia University, believes that "Emotional and personality factors are intertwined in depression so it's not really surprising that some type of personality change would accompany improvement in this condition" (Bowe 359). Similarly, psychiatrist Peter Kramer in his book *Listening to Prozac* claims, "Prozac offers nothing less than self transformation, turning self-doubts into confidence, increasing energy, even improving one's business acumen" (94).

In other cases, doctors have reported side effects of a more serious nature. Some scientists suspect that Prozac may accelerate tumor growth in people who already have cancer. In July 1992, the journal *Cancer Research* published a paper by a group of researchers, which showed that tumors in mice and rats seemed to grow faster when the animals were given Prozac (Nichols 40).

Prozac's other reported unpleasant side effects include jumpiness, nausea, insomnia, unwanted weight gain, headaches, and rapid heart beat. "These symptoms have appeared in hundreds of thousands of patients," said Peter R. Breggin, MD, author of *"Another View: Talking Back to Prozac."* He adds, "When a doctor prescribes Prozac, it should be understood that these symptoms exist and that the risk is quite high. I believe that these warnings go unsaid as millions of people continue to take Prozac" (Brown 153-5).

Controversy about SSRIs' side effects flared into national prominence in 2005 when they and older antidepressants were shown to double the risk of suicidal thoughts and behavior in children and adolescents. That discovery prompted the FDA to put a stern "black box" warning on package inserts. The warning cautions doctors to monitor young patients closely in their first months on SSRIs. Further, in June 2004, following actions taken by British drug authorities, the FDA released a statement recommending that physicians refrain from prescribing Paxil to new patients under 18. http://www.thenation.com/doc/20040105/degrandpre

Prozac is now the most frequently prescribed psychiatric medication. Physicians, mostly non-psychiatrists, are now writing almost one million prescriptions a month for the drug. "Many medical experts worry that some doctors are over-prescribing

Prozac and using it to treat relatively trivial disorders" (Nichols 36).

In addition to over-prescribing, there are problems with using Prozac as a quick-fix remedy. Psychiatrist Peter Breggin, cited earlier, said, "Too many doctors prescribe Prozac for minor depression or anxiety without talking to patients long enough to understand their problems. Too many patients look for pills to smooth out the inevitable ups and downs of everyday life" (Breggin 46-8). Breggin argues, "In looking for the quick-fix, too many psychiatrists have forgotten the importance of love, hope, and empathy in maintaining sanity." He adds, "The main problem is Prozac is merely a stimulant that does not get to the root of depression and is dangerous when used improperly" (Breggin 80).

Over time, Prozac's dark side is becoming more apparent to the medical community and eventually to the general public. Maybe Prozac isn't a wonder drug after all. While Prozac may help some people, it is not a miracle cure.

Works Cited

Bauer, Bruce. "Antidepressants May Alter Personality." *Science News*. June 4, 1994: 359.

Bowe, Claudia D. "Women and Depression: Are We Being Overdosed?" *Redbook*. March, 1992: 42-4.

Breggin, Peter. "Another View: Talking Back to Prozac." *Psychology Today*. July/August, 1994: 46-81.

—— *Talking Back to Prozac*. New York: St. Martin's Press, 1994.

Brown, Avery. "Miracle Worker." *People Weekly*. November 15, 1993: 153-5.

Kramer, Peter. *Listening to Prozac*. New York: Penguin, 1993.

Nichols, Mark. "Questioning Prozac." *McLean's*. May 23, 1994: 36-41.

"Open Verdict: Prozac and Suicide." *The Economist*. January 19, 1991: 76.

Richard Grandpre. "Trouble in Prozac Nation." *The Nation*. January 5, 2004. Retrieved October 11, 2006, from http://www.thenation.com/doc/20040105/degrandpre.

Stipp, David. "Trouble in Prozac." *Fortune*. November 28, 2005. Retrieved October 10, 2006, from http://money.cnn.com/magazines/fortune/fortune_archive/2005/11/28/8361973/index.htm

Model #2: Comics and History

Thesis: The development of comic books reflected the social situations of the twentieth century.

  I. 1930s: Comics offer escapism from the Depression.
     A. Escapist fantasies fuel comic strips.
     B. Comic strips compiled into books.
     C. Golden Age of Comics began.
 II. 1940-1945: Comics serve as American propaganda in World War II.
     A. WW II brings to escapism, reflected in comics.
     B. Comics feature patriotic heroes fighting for American values.
III. 1946-1950: Comics languished.
     A. The atomic bomb eclipsed superheroes' impact.
     B. Archie comics become popular with America's teenagers.
     C. Horror comics appear; become increasingly gory.
 IV. 1950-1955: Comics fall prey to Congressional attack.
     A. Congress meets to determine if juvenile delinquency caused by comics.
     B. Comics Code Authority formed to censor objectionable material in comics.
  V. 1956-1960s: Superheroes return to comics.
     A. New superheroes mirror American quest for heroes.
     B. War comics show civilian side of conflict, reflecting America's conflicted feelings about the Vietnam War.

VI. 1970s: Comics again became relevant.
   A. Comics focus on important issues in the 1970s.
   B. Comics become more gritty and realistic.
VII. 1990s: Comics reflect modern concerns.
   A. Comics keyed to pressing social issues.
   B. Comics similar to TV and movies in themes
      and topics.

Comics and History

During the 1930s, purveyors of popular culture offered escape to the American people. Their efforts served in part to ease people through the economic calamity of the Depression. Comic strips such as "Tarzan," "Buck Rogers," and "Prince Valiant" served to transport the reader else-where—a jungle, a desert, a distant planet, the past or the future—where the action had no bearing on the grueling reality of the day. As the decade progressed, adventure strips grew in popularity, fueling escapist fantasies for the economically distressed (Savage 3).

The comic book industry began in the mid-1930s. Publisher M.C. "Max" Gaines thought that compiling a collection of newspaper comic strips in a maga-zine form would work well as a premium giveaway (Thomson 23). So the first comic book was just that, reprints, given away with products ranging from soap to breakfast cereal to children's shoes. Other companies quickly saw the popularity of such magazines and very soon, all the usable strips were being reprinted and sold as books (Savage 4).

In 1934, Major Malcolm Wheeler-Nicholson start-ed his company by printing *New Comics* and *New Fun Comics*, using all new material. He hired Max Gaines to be in charge. In 1936, they started another new title, *Detective Comics*, the first comic book devoted to a single theme. These were precursors to the vaunted "Golden Age" of comic books.

The so-called "Golden Age" of comics officially began in 1938. While looking for a lead feature to launch another new title, Gaines and his editors settled on a strip that had been created five years earlier and unsuccessfully offered as a newspaper strip by two teenagers from Cleveland, Jerry Seigel and Joe Shuster. The character could lift cars, leap over buildings, and bounce bullets of his chest. The new magazine was named *Action Comics*. The character was called Superman (Daniels 32).

Superman proved to be an overnight success. As quickly as they could, other publishers--and DC itself, as Gaines' company had come to be called--sought to make economic lightning strike again and again. Costumed heroes arrived by the busload, feeding the escapist public with fantastic adventures (Savage 17).

Not long before the second World War, impelled by world affairs and the public mood, the comic-book industry created a number of "patriotic" heroes. Captain America, Fighting Yank, The Americommando, and even Uncle Sam, who began appearing in *National Comics* in July of 1940. This signaled the end of comic book escapism. As war became part of everyday life, comics became a vehicle for propaganda.

Military Comics was launched several months before the United States entered World War II, advertising "Stories of the Army and Navy." The leading hero was Blackhawk who, we learned in the first issue, was a Polish aviator whose family had been killed by Nazis. He waged aerial guerrilla warfare against Nazi Germany in his distinctive Blackhawk plane--which had a striking resemblance to a Grumman skyrocket (Goulart 181).

Comic books became a part of the Allied propaganda machine, emphasizing the need for a maximum war effort by portraying the enemy as a vast, inhuman evil. All variety of heroes, including Superman and Batman, were portrayed on covers promoting war bonds and punching out the "JapaNazis." Additionally, hundreds of thousands of comics were shipped to Allied troops around the world (Savage 10). The audience for comics grew to astounding proportions (Goulart 241).

After the war, however, interest in the superheroes began to wane. The atomic bomb was so overwhelming that costumed strongmen no longer seemed "super" to the American public. As a result, the comics' publishers started looking for new genres that would sell. Crime comics, western comics, war comics, and romance comics all started appearing. Like post-war Americans, comics had entered an age of complacency.

MLJ Publications started a back-up feature about "America's Typical Teenager"... a red-haired Romeo named Archie Andrews. Archie and his pals—Betty, Veronica, and Jughead—were America's stereotypical teenagers, sweet and carefree. They had typical 1950s concerns: finding dates, buying "cool" clothes, and getting Archie's jalopy to run. Archie eventually pushed all MLJ's super-heroes off the stands, which showed how 1950s teens favored comics that reflected the lighthearted mood of their everyday lives.

At the same time, EC Publications (which Max Gaines had started after leaving DC and which was now being run by his son Bill) started grinding out horror comics (Daniels 79). Clearly, they were catering to different audiences. With such titles as *Tales From the Crypt* and *Weird Science*, Bill Gaines and his crew set the industry scrambling in a new direction, one that eventually spawned a parental uproar and a Congressional investigation.

With each new rival publisher going for more and more gory material, it was an easy task for psychologist Fredric Wertham to blame all the ills of society on comic books. He gained notoriety and generated healthy sales of his book *Seduction of the Innocent*. Wertham's efforts spurred Congress to divert their attention briefly from Communism on the issue of juvenile delinquency. Congress viewed comics as a medium exclusively for children. Since the comics were very violent, they would therefore have to be altered to conform to Congress' narrow views of acceptable reading material (Daniels 83).

Congress's attempt to clamp down on comics reflects the general conservative attitude of the 1950s, the country's fear of "subversives" and strangers. Their "witch hunt" against comics is a variation of their "witch hunt" against Communists.

In an attempt to forestall Congressional action and public backlash, the larger publishers banded together and formed the Comics Magazine Association, with a Comics Code for appropriate comic book material. Like the blacklisted "Communists," Gaines and his competitors were forced to abandon comics virtually overnight--Gaines himself was called before the Senate Judiciary Subcommittee during the aforementioned hearings on juvenile delinquency. Gaines did, however, continue on the fringe of the business, publishing a highly successful comic book-turned-magazine to dodge the code: *MAD* (Daniels 85).

Comic books languished throughout the early and mid-50's until Julius Schwartz, an editor at

DC in 1956, proposed bringing the super-heroes back for another try. This was not a return to the escapism of the 1930s, though. These new heroes would be thoroughly modern --"more human," claimed the publishers. Schwartz revised and revamped DC's old lineup, including The Flash, Green Lantern, Hawkman, The Atom, and the Justice League of America (Crawford 326).

In part, these mythical heroes filled the need and desire for real heroes, a role filled by baseball players Joe DiMaggio and Jackie Robinson, movie stars John Wayne and Charlton Heston, and military figure Dwight David Eisenhower.

Meanwhile, over at Atlas (formerly Timely) Comics, publisher Martin Goodman saw the success of his rivals and suggested to his young editor that they should start publishing super-hero comics as well. The editor, a long-time writer of comics for Timely/Atlas named Stan Lee, took a shot and created the Fantastic Four, Spider-Man, the Incredible Hulk, and the X-Men (Crawford 340).

It should be mentioned, however, that for many years these new superhero comics were not as reflective of American society as their predecessors had been. The early sixties saw almost as many new comic book characters as the 1940s had, but while 1940s heroes protected the homefront in World War II, 1960s heroes scarcely, if ever, mentioned Vietnam (Savage 66).

As the Vietnam War escalated, the popularity of war comics decreased, with the notable exception of comics that showed the gritty, unglamorous side of war. The DC comic *Enemy Ace*, for example, described World War I from the vantage point of a

German pilot, thus humanized the enemy. The previous
generation of war comics, in contrast, had portrayed
war from the soldier's point of view. The Sergeant
Rock stories continued this new trend, focusing much
more on human relations than on the patriotic spirit
of World War II comics. By the end of the Vietnam
War, the only war comic left was Sgt. Rock. But like
any other old soldier, he eventually faded away.

In the early 1970s, DC had another brief period
of historical relevance as the new generation of
writers combined journalism with fiction. "Not
fact, not current events presented in panel art,
but fantasy rooted in the issues of the day," said
Denny O'Neil, a comic author of that time, describing these new comics. These angry issues dealt with
racism, overpopulation, pollution, and drug addic-
tion. DC dramatized the drug abuse problem in an
unusual and unprecedented way by showing Green
Arrow's heretofore clean-cut boy sidekick Speedy
turning into a heroin addict. These comics clearly
show America's concern with the pressing social
issues of the day. While DC was showered with
praise for this bold move, declining sales caused
Schwartz to announce in 1973, "Relevance is
dead." (Goulart 297)

Also in the 1970s, the comic book industry
became aware that their audience was changing.
Instead of losing all its readers at age 14 (as
had been the pattern in the past), they were stay-
ing on, looking for more diverse and challenging
material. Coupled with the growth of a direct market, in which the publishers could supply books
directly to specialized comic book shops, and the
utilization of new printing technologies, the

industry went through its largest expansion with record numbers of titles being produced every month (Goulart 307). As America became more open about previously-taboo subjects -- sex and violence-- comics became much more gritty and realistic.

Today's comics deal with important issues on a new level. Timely/Atlas, now called Marvel Comics, dealt with racism in a whole new way. After they established that their heroes were "Mutants," they ran a crossover series about the mutant hate groups that had sprung up in the comic-book world. Cries of "Die Mutie scum!" echoed through the comics with an almost Ku Klux Klan-worthy fervor (Goulart 332).

A new generation of horror comics, many produced by fans-turned-professionals from England, began to appear, aimed at an adult audience. Far more graphic than those of the 1950s, but also with far more complex storylines, these books in particular have led former readers back into the comic book fold. This echoes the way television and movies have changed to fit the public's taste over the past forty years (Goulart 344). DC's Vertigo line, targets the same audience as the TV show *Buffy the Vampire Slayer*.

Over the years, as society as changed, so have comics. Now, as the world becomes increasingly computerized, comic companies have web page. In addition, most of the larger comic companies are coloring on computer rather than by hand. As the world continues to change, the comic book industry must continue to adapt to fit the needs and wants of its audience if it is to survive.

Works Cited

Crawford, Hubert H. *Crawford's Encyclopedia of Comic Books*. Middle Village, NY.: Comicade Enterprises, 1978.

Daniels, Les. *COMIX: A History of Comic Books in America*. New York. Bonanza Books, 1971.

Goulart, Ron. *Great History of Comic Books*. Chicago, Illinois. Contemporary Books, Inc. 1986.

Savage, William W. *Comic Books and America, 1945-1954*. Oklahoma city Okla. University of Oklahoma Press, 1990.

Thomson, Don. *The Comic-Book Book*. New Rochelle, NY. Arlington House, 1973.

Index

Index